Long A Sound: ai

The Great Longo is a magician.
He makes long vowel words!

Add long **a** words to his magic chain.
Look at each picture.
Write the letters **ai** on the lines.
Say the word.
Write the words in the magic chain.

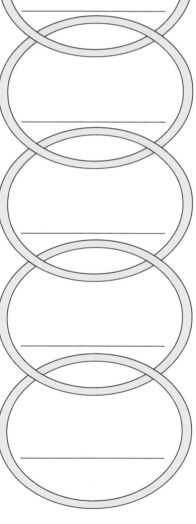

1.

s __ __ l

2.

sn __ __ l

3.

r __ __ n

4.

n __ __ l

5.

tr __ __ n

6.

p __ __ l

Long A Sound: ay

Make a long **a** playhouse! Make it with **ay** bricks!

Look at each picture.
Write the letters **ay** on the lines.
Say the word.
Write one long **a** word on each brick of the playhouse.

1.

h __ __

2.

spr __ __

3.
pl __ __

4.
j __ __

5.
tr __ __

6.

cr __ __ on

Long A Sound: eigh

The Great Longo had a long **a** party.
He called it the **sleigh** ride party.

Use the **eigh** words to finish the sentences.
Then read the story to find out what happened.

eight	**eighty-eight**
Neigh	**weigh**
sleigh	**Eight**

The Great Longo took __ __ __ __ __ of his friends on a

__ __ __ __ __ __ ride. "What did your horse say?" one of

his friends asked. "__ __ __ __ __ ," said Longo. Another

friend asked, "How much does your horse __ __ __ __ __ ?"

"__ __ __ __ __ hundred __ __ __ __ __ - __ __ __ __ __

pounds," said Longo.

Long A Sound: silent e

The Great Longo has a silent **e** wand!
The silent **e** wand changes words.

Many words with a long vowel sound
are spelled with a vowel, a consonant
and then **e**.

m**a**d**e**

Add an **e** to the **bold** word to make a long **a** word.
Read each sentence.

1. The **man** was on a horse with a nice ___ ___ ___ ___ .

2. He hit the **can** with his ___ ___ ___ ___ .

3. Which **hat** do you ___ ___ ___ ___ ?

4. The magician's **cap** matched his ___ ___ ___ ___ .

Long A Sound: silent e

The Great Longo is still making long **a** words with the silent **e** wand.

Write a long **a** word from each **bold** word in the sentence.
Read the sentence.

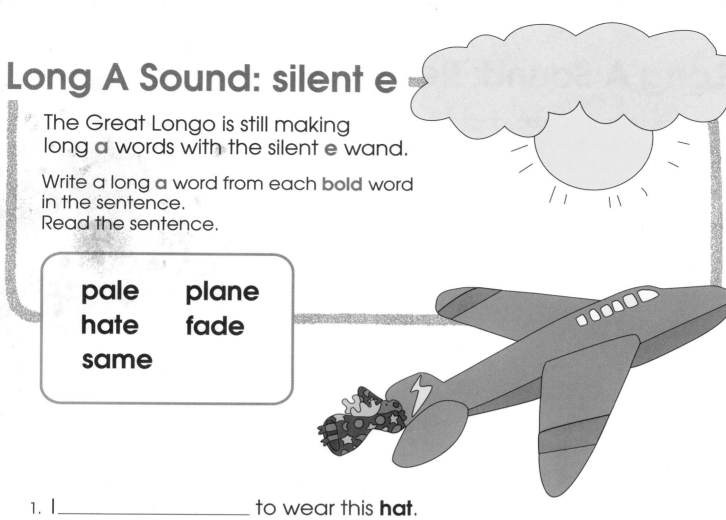

pale	**plane**
hate	**fade**
same	

1. I _____ to wear this **hat**.

2. My **pal** looked sick and _____ .

3. **Sam** is on the _____ team as Joe.

4. I **plan** to fly on a _____ .

5. It is a **fad** to _____ jeans.

Long A Sound: Review

Color each long **a** word blue.
Then see what you find!

wall far pop red art time

roar in say red to

ran blue play pail sew

cat home plane sad cane soap

pup eight cake tail man

ten train ask me weigh be

Long A Sound: Review

The Great Longo is on the long **a** train.

Fill the train cars with long **a** words.
Write only the long **a** words on the cars of the train.

stay	car	made	pail
hat	ask	bake	mad
ran	day	sad	bat

ran

pail

Long E Sound: ee

The Great Longo has a friend to help you with the long **e** sound. His name is Buzzing Bee.

Write the correct long **e** word by each picture. Say the word.

sheep	**teeth**
three	**teepee**
wheel	**tree**

1.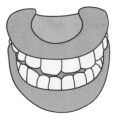

_____

2.

_____

3.

_____

4.

_____

5.

Sheep

6.

_____

Long E Sound: ea

Sometimes the letters **ea** make the long **e** sound.
Look at each picture.
Write **ea** on the lines.
Say the word.

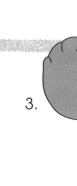

1.  m __ __ t

2.  l __ __ f

3. s __ __ l

4. 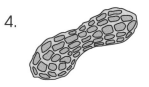 p __ __ nut

5.  __ __ gle

6. j __ __ ns

7. b __ __ k

8. b __ __ ds

Long E Sound: ey

The Great Longo makes magic with the letters **ey**.

Write a long **e** word by adding the missing letters **ey**.
Say the word.
Draw a line from the picture to the word.

Look at all of these long **e** words made with **ey**!

1. **k** ___ ___

2. **monk** ___ ___

3. **donk** ___ ___

4. **hock** ___ ___

5. **mon** ___ ___

6. **turk** ___ ___

Long E Sound: ie, e

Help the Great Longo catch a thief!

Write the correct word by each picture.
Say the word.
Listen for the long e sound.

he	field	chief
she	shield	thief
	cookie	

Long E Sound: Review

The Great Longo is hiding things!

Circle a hidden picture for each long **e** word.

cookie	key	peanut	bee	turkey
teepee	tree	wheel	leaf	penny

Long E Sound: Review

Look at each picture.
Say the word.
Circle **Yes** if the word has a long e sound.
Circle **No** if it does not.

1.
thief
Yes   No

2.
sheep
Yes   No

3.
bed
Yes   No

4.
peach
Yes   No

5.
net
Yes   No

6.
feet
Yes   No

7.
men
Yes   No

8.
bee
Yes   No

9.
monkey
Yes   No

Long I Sound: ie, y

The Great Longo makes long **i** words. He uses the letter **y** or the letters **ie**. The Great Longo is tricky!

Read each sentence.
Then fill in the blanks with the paired words that rhyme.
Use the words in the box.

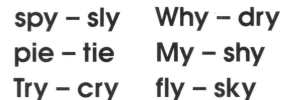

spy – sly	Why – dry
pie – tie	My – shy
Try – cry	fly – sky

1. Birds _____ in the _____ .

2. A _____ must be very _____ .

3. _____ sister is very _____ .

4. _____ not let our paintings _____ ?

5. Some _____ fell on my _____ .

6. _____ not to _____ .

Long I Sound: igh

Mighty Lion is chasing the Great Longo.

Help him get away. Write the
correct word by each picture.

night	knight	light
fight	fright	right
	high	

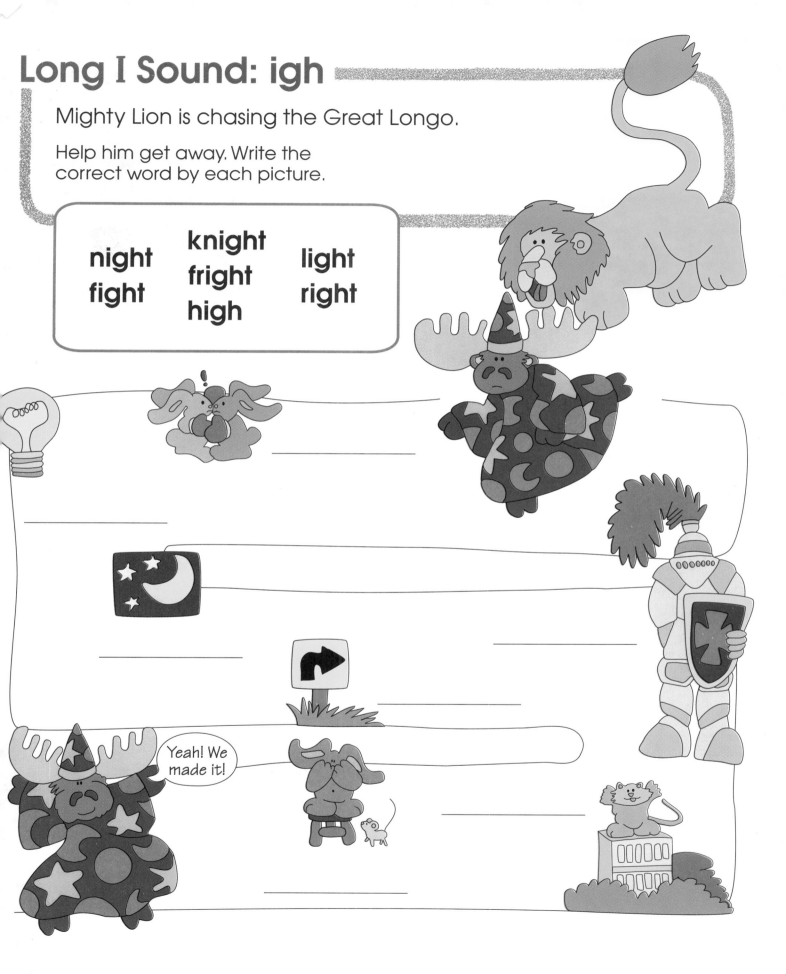

Yeah! We
made it!

Long I Sound: ild, ind

The Great Longo is making riddles.
The answers are long i words that end in ild or ind.

Read each sentence.
Write the correct long i word.

blind	mind
wild	find
child	kind

1. If you help people, you are _____ .

2. A baby is a _____ .

3. I think with my _____ .

4. If you can't see, you are _____ .

5. If you lose a toy, you try to _____ it.

6. A horse that is not tame is _____ .

Long I Sound: silent e

The Great Longo is making silent **e** words again!
This time his words have the long **i** sound.

Write a long **i** word by adding the missing **i**.
Say the word.
Draw a line from each word to its picture.

1. **d __ me**

2. **t __ me**

3. **b __ ke**

4. **k __ te**

5. **wr __ te**

6. **t __ re**

7. **f __ re**

8. **h __ ve**

Long I Sound: Review

Help the Great Longo on a long **i** butterfly chase!

Catch all the long **i** butterflies!
Color each butterfly that has a long **i** word on it.

Long I Sound: Review

Read each word or say each picture word.
Circle the word or picture in each row that has a long i sound.

1.

2. **nine** **eight** **six**

3.

4. **gift** **tire** **dig**

5.

6. **baby** **bee** **dime**

7.

Long O Sound: oe, oa

The Great Longo makes long **o** words in many tricky ways.
Sometimes he uses **oe** to make the long **o** sound.
Sometimes he uses **oa** to make the long **o** sound.

Look at each picture.
Write in the missing letters.
Say the word.

1. t __ __

2. h __ __

3. d __ __

4. r __ __ d

5. c __ __ t

6. t __ __ st

7. b __ __ t

8. g __ __ t

9. t __ __ d

Long O Sound: o, ow, old, ost

The Great Longo is making long **o** sentences.
He makes the long **o** sound with **o**, **ow**, **old**, or **ost**.
How tricky!

Read each sentence.
Write the correct long **o** word.

no	ghost	bowl
go	snow	Gold
old	crow	

1. Get ready, get set, _____ !

2. I eat soup from a _____ .

3. White _____ fell from the sky.

4. _____ is bright and shiny.

5. Did you see a _____ on Halloween?

6. That black bird is a _____ .

7. If it's not yes, it is _____ .

8. How _____ are you?

Long O Sound: silent e

The Great Longo is lost! He wants to go home.
Help him find the way.

Draw a line from the Great Longo to
the first word that has the long o sound.
Then draw a line to connect all of the
words with the long o sound.

nose

rope

log

pop

cop

notes

pole

bone

dog

on

hole

mop

hop

rose

home

Long O Sound: Review

Help the Great Longo put long o words inside his giant globe!

Look at the words in the box.
Write only the words that contain the long o sound inside Longo's giant globe.
Let's go!

globe	told	rope
know	rode	note
now	row	not
goat	top	got
home	toe	lot

Long O Sound: Review

The Great Longo has a secret message waiting for you!

Color each box that has a long o word.

night	bump	sip	log	is
jump		cat	chip	date
rate	bowl	dog	be	hose
	go	hoe		
	so	it		be	hat	
globe	row	lip	hat	
	roll	old	late	he
low	lot	she	ship	no	rode	toe	own
goat	blow			
knee	hop	dip	light	hip	skate
	nice	save		stop
ice	son	great	bee	not

Longo's secret message reads: _____

Long U Sound: silent e, ui, ew, ue

Draw a line from the long u word to the correct picture.
Then write the word next to the picture.

tube

1. _____

suit

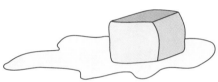

2. _____

cube

3. _____

fuel

4. _____

glue

5. _____

screw

6. _____

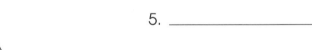

Long U Sound: Review

Help the Great Longo make
sentences with long **u** words.

Write the correct long **u** word on each line.

mew	**few**	**cute**
huge	**view**	**use**

1. If there aren't many, there are _____ .

2. I heard the kitten _____ .

3. I thought that baby was very _____ .

4. An elephant is a _____ animal.

5. Standing on a mountain, you have a nice _____ .

6. When you work with something, you _____ it.

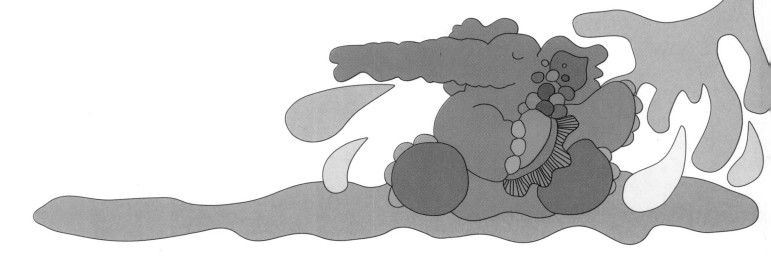

Long Vowel Sounds: General Review

Circle the word in each row that has the
same long vowel sound as the **bold** word.

1. **mule**   lip   fuel   hot

2. **go**   clam   nut   post

3. **chief**   milk   me   fun

4. **five**   sky   stick   gift

5. **cane**   way   fan   end

6. **leave**   step   key   miss

7. **know**   fast   float   dock

8. **rice**   mile   trick   dish

Long Vowel Sounds: General Review

Let's color Longo!

Use the sound key to color the big picture of Longo.

Long **a** – blue
Long **e** – orange
Long **i** – purple
Long **o** – brown
Long **u** – yellow

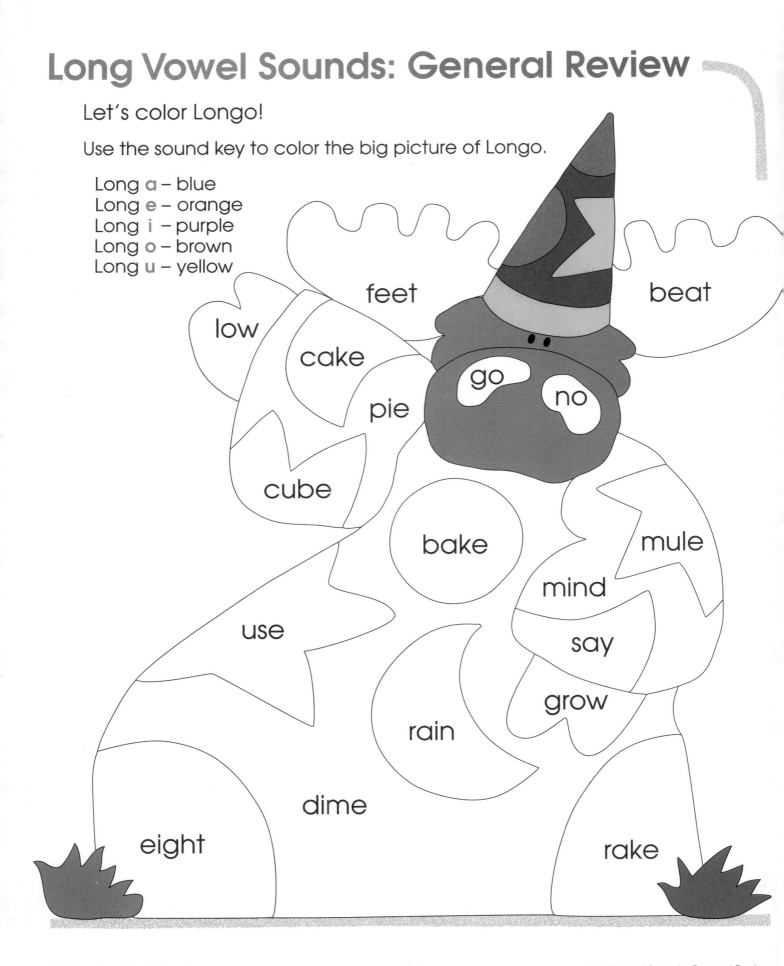

feet

beat

low

cake

go

no

pie

cube

bake

mule

mind

use

say

grow

rain

dime

eight

rake

Long Vowel Sounds: General Review

The Great Longo is playing long vowel opposites.
You can play too!

Read each word.
Write a long vowel word
that means the opposite!

take	sleep	low	sweet
dry	clean	go	white
over	cold	me	night

1. **dirty** _ _ _ _ _

2. **hot** _ _ _ _

3. **sour** _ _ _ _ _

4. **you** _ _ _

5. **black** _ _ _ _ _

6. **under** _ _ _ _

7. **day** _ _ _ _

8. **wake** _ _ _ _ _

9. **come** _ _

10. **give** _ _ _ _

11. **wet** _ _ _

12. **high** _ _ _

Long Vowel Sounds: General Review

Say each word.
Draw a line from the word to
the long vowel sound you hear.

1. **sheep**

 2. **eight**

3. **gold**

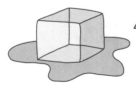 4. **cube**

5. **try**

Long
a

Long
e

Long
i

Long
o

Long
u

6. **chief**

7. **goat**

8. **blue**

9. **wild**

10. **cane**

Long Vowel Sounds: General Review

Find all the long vowel words.
Color them green.
Then read Longo's secret message.

fog	log	had	thumb	bun	dance
sit	clock	bet	jump	pet
	know	run	set	thief	cake
let	nice	is	lit	no	
go	if	ice	hike	hill
rice	glue	at	say	
cute	seen	pie	rake	mean
sock	it	had	met	dog
jog	has	net	not	hit	sun	bit	mad
			fun	

Longo's secret message reads: _____

Answer Key

Page 33
1. sail
2. snail
3. rain
4. nail
5. train
6. pail

Page 34
1. hay
2. spray
3. play
4. jay
5. tray
6. crayon

Page 35
1. eight
2. sleigh
3. Neigh
4. weigh
5. Eight
6. eighty-eight

Page 36
1. mane
2. cane
3. hate
4. cape

Page 37
1. hate
2. pale
3. same
4. plane
5. fade

Page 38
say, play, pail, plane, cane, eight, cake, tail, train, weigh

Page 39
stay, made, pail, bake, day

Page 40
1. teeth
2. tree
3. wheel
4. teepee
5. sheep
6. three

Page 41
1. meat
2. leaf
3. seal
4. peanut
5. eagle
6. jeans
7. beak
8. beads

Page 42
1. key
2. monkey
3. donkey
4. hockey
5. money
6. turkey

Page 43
shield, chief, he, she, field, cookie, thief

Page 44
Automatic fill-in.

Page 45
1. yes
2. yes
3. no
4. yes
5. no
6. yes
7. no
8. yes
9. yes

Page 46
1. fly, sky
2. spy, sly
3. My, shy
4. Why, dry
5. pie, tie
6. Try, cry

Page 47
fight, light, night, right, knight, high, fright

Page 48
1. kind
2. child
3. mind
4. blind
5. find
6. wild

Page 49
dime, time, bike, kite, write, tire, fire, hive

Page 50
bike, lie, sight, write, might, fire, pie, wife, sky, ice

Page 51
1. fly
2. nine
3. bike
4. tire
5. hive
6. dime
7. five

Page 52
1. toe
2. hoe
3. doe
4. road
5. coat
6. toast
7. boat
8. goat
9. toad

Page 53
1. go
2. bowl
3. snow
4. Gold
5. ghost
6. crow
7. no
8. old

Page 54
nose, rope, pole, notes, bone, hole, rose, home

Page 55
globe, told, rope, know, rode, note, row, goat, home, toe

Page 56
globe, low, row, bowl, so, roll, goat, go, old, blow, hoe, no, rode, hose, toe, own, **(HELLO)**

Page 57
1. glue
2. cube
3. screw
4. fuel
5. suit
6. tube

Page 58
1. few
2. mew
3. cute
4. huge
5. view
6. use

Page 59
1. fuel
2. post
3. me
4. sky
5. way
6. key
7. float
8. mile

Page 60
Automatic fill-in.

Page 61
1. clean
2. cold
3. sweet
4. me
5. white
6. over
7. night
8. sleep
9. go
10. take
11. dry
12. low

Page 62
1. long e
2. long a
3. long o
4. long u
5. long i
6. long e
7. long o
8. long u
9. long i
10. long a

Page 63
rice, cute, know, go, seen, nice, glue, pie, ice, thief, rake, hike, no, say, mean, cake, **(LONGO)**

Short Vowel Sounds: a

Alli Gator likes to act. She uses props.
Props help a play to seem real.

The following pictures are short **a** props for her play.
Write in the missing letters for each picture.

1. __ a __

2. __ a __

3. __ __ ck

4. st __ mp

5. b __ t

6. l __ mp

7. __ a __

8. __ a __

9. __ __ sk

Short Vowel Sounds: a

People sing and dance in some plays.
Alli tap-dances to short **a** words.

Look at each picture. Say the word.
Circle **yes** if the word has a short **a** sound.
Circle **no** if the word does not have the short **a** sound.

1. Yes   No   2. Yes   No   3. Yes   No

4. Yes   No   5. Yes   No   6. Yes   No

7. Yes   No   8. Yes   No   9. Yes   No

10. Yes   No   11. Yes   No   12. Yes   No

Review: short a

Stage lights help us to see props and players better.

Color the short **a** words red to see what is on stage.

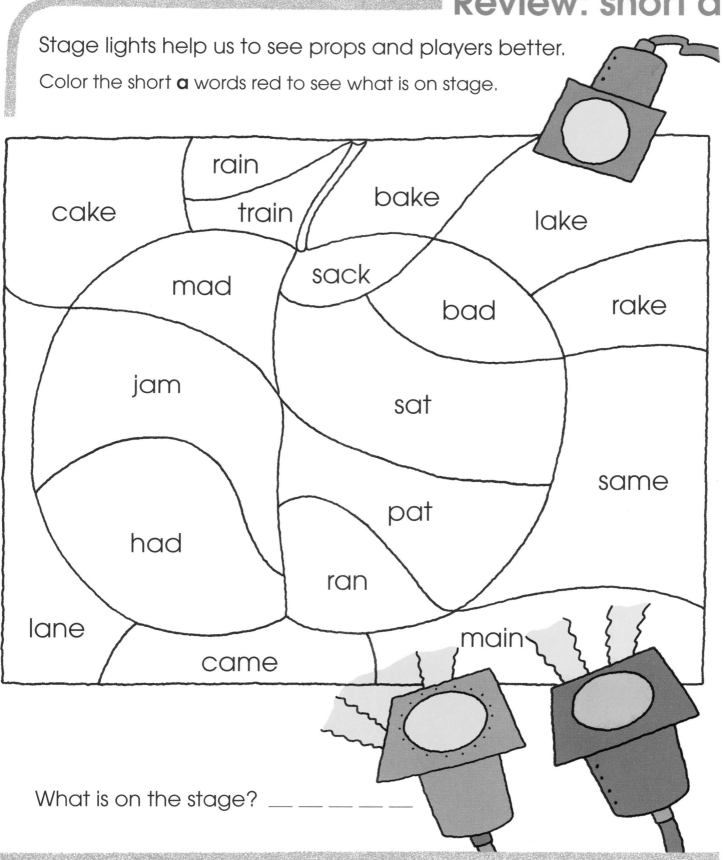

rain

cake

train

bake

lake

mad

sack

bad

rake

jam

sat

same

had

pat

ran

lane

main

came

What is on the stage? __ __ __ __ __ __ __

Review: short a

Alli is reading the script for the short **a** play. Some words are missing.

Write each answer on the correct line.

mask   tag   bat
hand   cat

1. PAT: Let's play baseball. I'll get the ball and _____ .

2. SALLY: If I want to be the catcher, I'll need to wear a _____ .

3. SALLY: My _____ will be our mascot.

4. PAT: I can catch the ball with this mitt on my _____ .

5. SALLY: And I will _____ runners to get the winning out!

Short Vowel Sounds: e

Elmer Elephant is in the short **e** play.
Help Elmer to learn his way around the stage.

Write the correct short **e** word by each picture.
This will get Elmer around the stage like a pro!

| tent | sled | ten |
| nest | bell | bed |

1. _____

4. _____ 3. _____

2. _____

5. _____

6. _____

Short Vowel Sounds: e

Help Elmer to remember his words for the short **e** play.

Draw a line from each short **e** word to its picture.
Write each word under its picture.
Say the word for Elmer.

web

1. __ __ __

belt

2. __ __ __

pen

dress

5. __ __ __ __

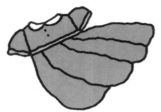

3. __ __ __

desk

hen

6. __ __ __

4. __ __ __ __

bed

7. __ __ __

Elmer does not know which words are his for the play.

Write an **e** by all of Elmer's short **e** words.
Put an **x** by the words that do not have the short **e** sound.

1. ___ **bell**

2. ___ **cent**

3. ___ **teeth**

4. ___ **web**

5. ___ **leaf**

6. ___ **red**

7. ___ **bee**

8. ___ **nest**

Review: short a, e

Alli and Elmer are in a play about fire safety.
Can you help them with their lines?

Read the sentence.
Write the correct answer on the line.
Use the words from the box.

plan	fast	handle	bell
red	get	ladder	Men

1. ELMER: It is time to put out a fire when the _____ rings.

2. ELMER: _____ and women firefighters save lives every day.

3. ALLI: We need to _____ when it comes to fire safety.

4. ALLI: You can hang a rope _____ from your window.

5. ALLI: And don't open a door if the _____ is hot!

6. ELMER: If you smell smoke, _____ help.

7. ELMER: Firefighters will come in their big, _____ truck.

8. ALLI: They will help you as _____ as they can.

Actors go to school, too.
Help Alli and Elmer to do their school lesson.

Write the correct short vowel **a** or **e** on the line.
Say the word. Then draw a line to its picture.

1. w __ b

2. f __ n

3. __ pple

4. __ nt

5. sl __ d

6. t __ nt

7. d __ sk

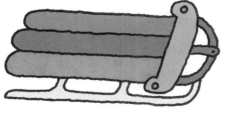

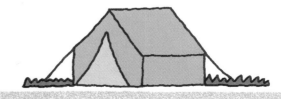

Short Vowel Sounds: i

Meet Iggy Iguana. He is writing his own short **i** play.
He needs help with some words.

Write the short **i** on the blank.
Say the word.

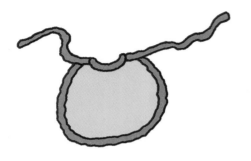

1. b __ b

2. f __ sh

3. p __ g

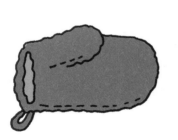

4. m __ tt

5. h __ ll

6. d __ sh

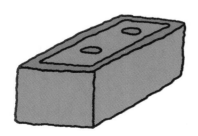

7. br __ ck

8. w __ g

9. g __ ft

Short Vowel Sounds: i

Iggy is practicing for the short **i** play.
He needs to practice with short **i** props.

Look at each picture. Say the word.
Circle **yes** if the word has the short **i** sound.
Circle **no** if the word does not have the short **i** sound.

1. Yes   No

2. Yes   No

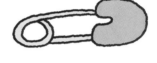

3. Yes   No

4. Yes   No

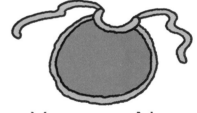

5. Yes   No

6. Yes   No

7. Yes   No

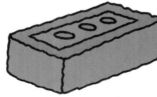

8. Yes   No

9. Yes   No

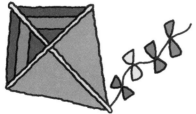

10. Yes   No

11. Yes   No

12. Yes   No

Short Vowel Sounds: i

Iggy wants you to see his short **i** play.

Color the letters with short **i** words to see what Iggy has for you.

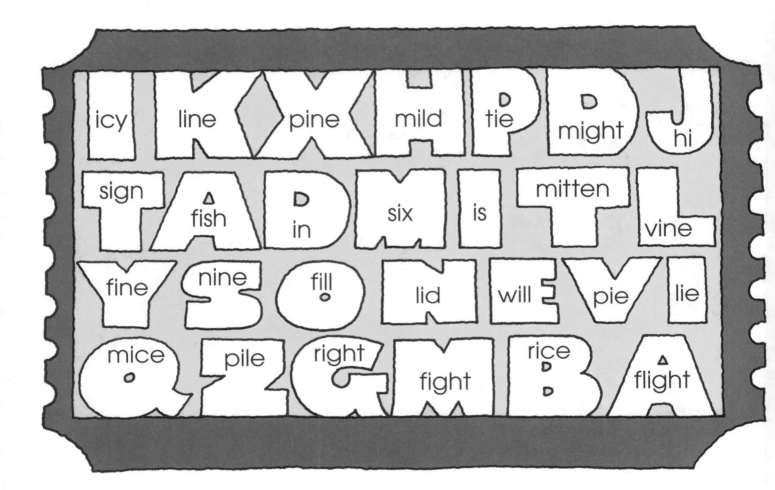

What is Iggy's message? __ __ __ __ __   __ __ __

Now you can go to the short **i** play!

Alli and Iggy have notes on their dressing-room doors.

Write all the short **a** words on Alli's door.
Write all the short **i** words on Iggy's door.

pig	hat	lamp	six
hill	hand	fish	bad

Review: short e, i

Actors need to know their words.
Help Iggy and Elmer to find the correct words.

Look at each picture. Say the word.
Draw a line from Iggy to each short **i** picture.
Draw a line from Elmer to each short **e** picture.

Elmer and Iggy are setting the stage.
Help them to find the six missing short vowel props.

Circle the hidden pictures.
Then write each short vowel word on the correct line below.

bat   pen   fan
gift   tent   fish

short a   **short e**   **short i**

_____   _____   _____

_____   _____   _____

79

Short Vowel Sounds: o

Meet Olive Octopus.
She has brought her own props for the short **o** play.

She forgets what she has. Write an **o** in each blank.
Then tell Olive what she is holding.

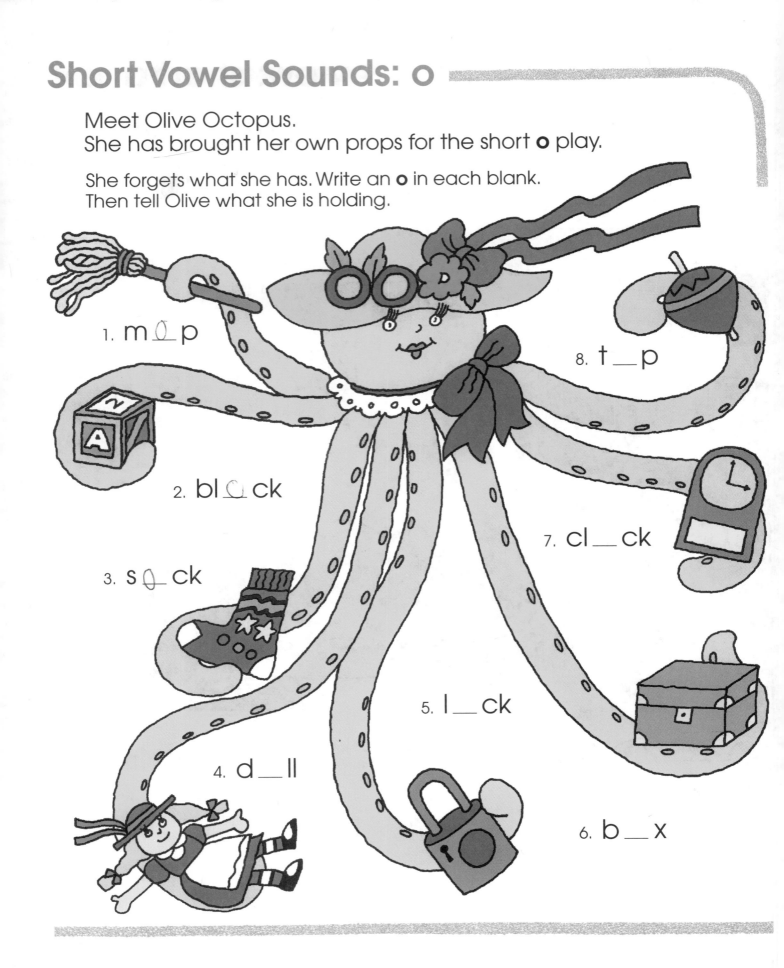

1. m o p

2. bl o ck

3. s o ck

4. d __ ll

5. l __ ck

6. b __ x

7. cl __ ck

8. t __ p

Olive dreams of singing in the play.
She is singing songs about short **o** words.

Circle the short **o** pictures to hear words from her song.

1.

2.

3.

4.

5.

6.

7.

Review: short o

Olive needs one more prop for the short **o** play.
Help her to find it.

Color all the short **o** words in the picture red.

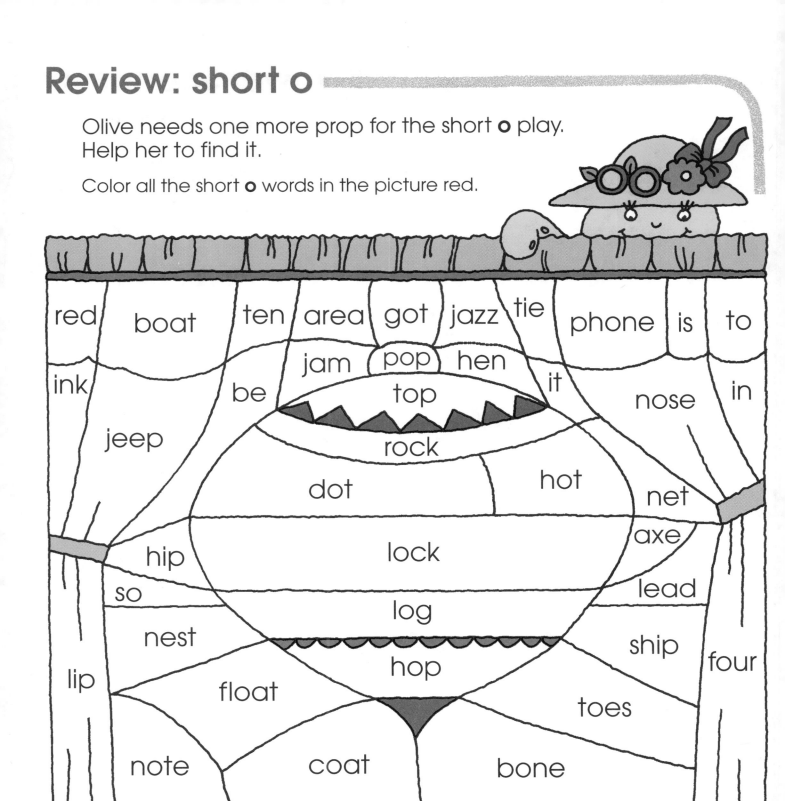

red | boat | ten | area | got | jazz | tie | phone | is | to

jam | pop | hen | it

ink | be | top | nose | in

jeep | rock

dot | hot | net

hip | lock | axe

so | lead

nest | log | ship

lip | hop | four

float | toes

note | coat | bone

What is the prop Olive needs? ___ ___ ___

Review: short a, o

Costumes are like props you wear to make a play seem real.

Answer the riddles about costumes.
Write **a** on the blank if the answer is a short **a** word.
Write **o** if the answer is a short **o** word.

1. You wear this on your head.   **h __ t**

2. Too many clothes make you feel this way.   **h __ t**

3. A kind of tall hat.   **t __ p**

4. A kind of dance shoe.   **t __ p**

5. You put this on your foot.   **s __ ck**

6. You carry things in it.   **s __ ck**

Review: short e, o

Oh, oh! Alli and Elmer are afraid to go on stage.
They are hiding with some props. Help the show to go on.

Circle the six hidden pictures.
Write each word on the correct line.

hen	bed	clock
sock	mop	bell

short e   **short o**

_____   _____

_____   _____

_____   _____

Review: short i, o

Sounds such as music help tell a story.

Look at the pictures and listen for the short vowel sound.
Circle **i** if the picture has the short **i** sound.
Circle **o** if it has the short **o** sound.

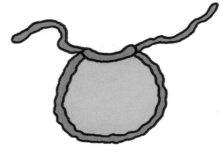

1. **i**   **o**

2. **i**   **o**

3. **i**   **o**

4. **i**   **o**

5. **i**   **o**

6. **i**   **o**

7. **i**   **o**

8. **i**   **o**

9. **i**   **o**

Review: short a, e, i, o

It is the last practice before the play opens.
Help the players with their words.

Circle the picture in each row that has
the same sound as the short vowel.

1. short **a**

2. short **e**

3. short **e**

4. short **i**

5. short **a**

6. short **o**

7. short **i**

8. short **o**

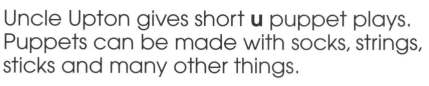

Uncle Upton gives short **u** puppet plays. Puppets can be made with socks, strings, sticks and many other things.

Look at the pictures of the short **u** puppets. Write the missing letter. Say the word.

This play moves short **u** puppets with strings.

1. d __ ck   2. b __ g   3. c __ b

This play moves short **u** puppets with sticks.

4. s __ b   5. b __ s   6. tr __ ck

Short Vowel Sounds: u

All players wear makeup when they are in a play.
Putting on makeup is like coloring.

Color the pictures with the short **u** sound.

1.

2.

3.

4.

5.

6.

7.

8.

9.

10.

11.

12.

Short Vowel Sounds: u

Upton will paint the background for the play.
Can you help him?

Color all of the short **u** words yellow.

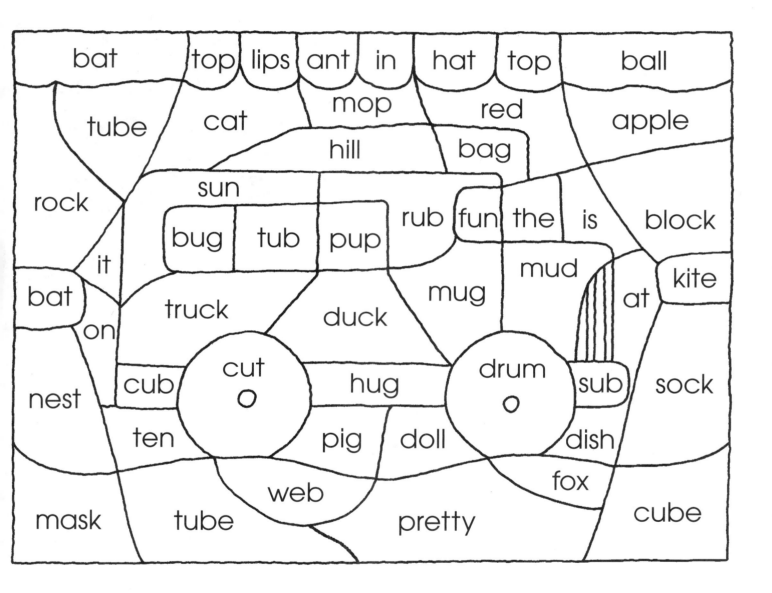

This is a picture of a ___ ___ ___ .

Review: short a, u

Alli and Upton are missing some words from their lines.

Write the correct words from the box on the lines to help them.

cap	bug	bag	cut
cat	fan	fun	cup

SETTING: Alli and Upton are in a shop trying to find a birthday present for Dad.

1. ALLI: Let's get Dad a baseball _____ .

2. UPTON: Maybe a _____ for his soup.

3. ALLI: Oh! Here is a picture of a _____ with kittens.

4. UPTON: Does Dad need a knife to _____ apples?

5. UPTON: This net would be good for _____ collecting.

6. ALLI: Mmm! We could get him a _____ of cookies.

7. ALLI: It's been hot. How about a _____ to keep cool?

8. UPTON: Let's get it all! Dad will really have a _____ birthday now.

When you go to a play, your ticket shows you where to sit.
Write the correct words on the seats.

Write short **e** words on the short **e** side.
Write short **u** words on the short **u** side.

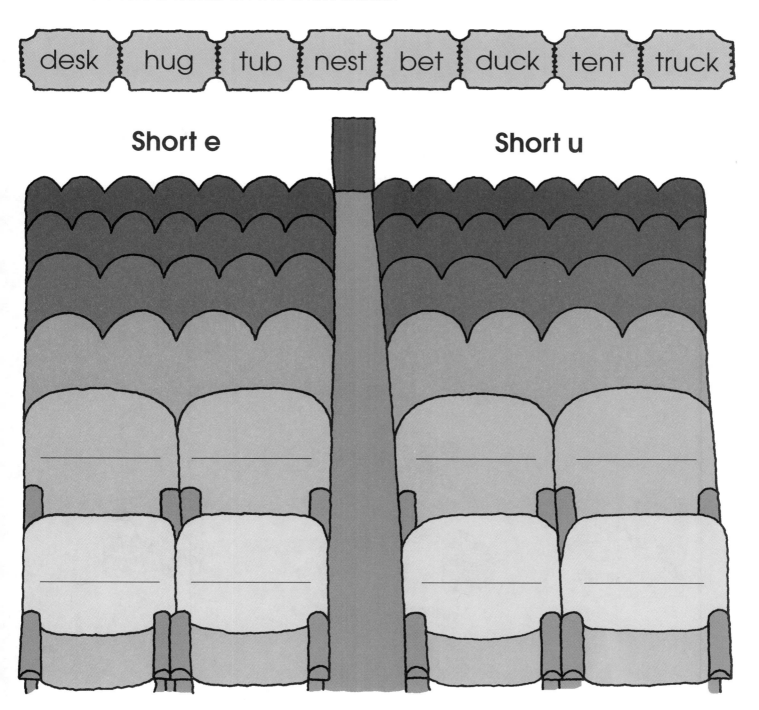

| desk | hug | tub | nest | bet | duck | tent | truck |

Short e   **Short u**

Review: short i, u

Places, everyone! Iggy and Upton find
their places, but they need their props.

Look at each picture. Say the word.
Write the correct short vowel **i** or **u** on the blank.
Draw a line from Iggy to each short **i** picture.
Draw a line from Upton to each short **u** picture.

1. p __ g

2. b __ s

3. m __ ttens

4. c __ p

5. f __ sh

6. dr __ m

Review: short o, u

Help Upton and Olive to find their way to the show.

Write the correct word by each picture.

doll   duck   bus

lock   mop   fox

1. _____

2. _____

3. _____

4. _____

5. _____

6. _____

Review: short a, e, i, o, u

It's opening night for the short vowel play! See what the play is about.

Look at each picture. Say the word. Circle the vowel that has the short vowel sound heard in the picture word.

Short Vowel Play

1. **e**　**a**

2. **e**　**i**

3. **i**　**o**

4. **o**　**u**

5. **e**　**a**

6. **e**　**o**

7. **e**　**i**

8. **e**　**u**

9. **i**　**o**

10. **i**　**u**

11. **e**　**a**

12. **i**　**e**

13. **o**　**u**

14. **o**　**a**

15. **o**　**e**

16. **o**　**i**

Would you like to make a short vowel play?

Cut out these short vowel players.
(Do this when you are done with the whole
book. The answer page is on the back.)
Get some glue and popsicle sticks.
Glue the sticks to the backs of the cutouts.
Now write your own play with short vowel words.
Invite your friends to see your new play. Have fun!

Have a grownup help you!

Answer Key

Page 65
1. hat
2. fan
3. tack
4. stamp
5. bat
6. lamp
7. cat
8. van
9. mask

Page 66
1. yes
2. no
3. yes
4. no
5. no
6. yes
7. yes
8. yes
9. no
10. yes
11. no
12. yes

Page 67
Automatic fill-in.
On stage: **apple**

Page 68
1. bat
2. mask
3. cat
4. hand
5. tag

Page 69
1. tent
2. bed
3. sled
4. bell
5. ten
6. nest

Page 70
1. dress
2. web
3. hen
4. belt
5. desk
6. bed
7. pen

Page 71
1. e
2. e
3. x
4. e
5. x
6. e
7. x
8. e

Page 72
1. bell
2. Men
3. plan
4. ladder
5. handle
6. get
7. red
8. fast

Page 73
1. web
2. fan
3. apple
4. ant
5. sled
6. tent
7. desk

Page 74
1. bib
2. fish
3. pig
4. mitt
5. hill
6. dish
7. brick
8. wig
9. gift

Page 75
1. yes
2. no
3. yes
4. no
5. no
6. yes
7. yes
8. yes
9. yes
10. no
11. yes
12. yes

Page 76
Automatic fill-in.
message: **ADMIT ONE**

Page 77
short **a**:
hat, lamp, hand, bad
short **i**:
pig, hill, fish, six

Page 78
short **e**:
dress, ten, bed, tent
short **i**:
lips, fish, bib, six

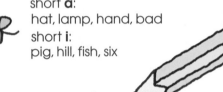

Page 79
short **a**:
bat, fan
short **e**:
pen, tent
short **i**:
gift, fish

Page 80
1. mop
2. block
3. sock
4. doll
5. lock
6. box
7. clock
8. top

Page 81
1. sock
2. clock
3. fox
4. top
5. mop
6. block
7. doll

Page 82
Automatic fill-in.
missing prop: **top**

Page 83
1. hat
2. hot
3. top
4. tap
5. sock
6. sack

Page 84
short **e**:
hen, bed, bell
short **o**:
sock, mop, clock

Page 85
1. i
2. o
3. o
4. i
5. o
6. i
7. o
8. i
9. o

Page 86
1. cat
2. belt
3. desk
4. pig
5. bat
6. lock
7. bib
8. mop

Page 87
1. duck
2. bug
3. cub
4. sub
5. bus
6. truck

Page 88
color:
2. sun
4. duck
5. drum
9. tub
10. cup
12. bug

Page 89
Automatic fill-in.
picture of: **bus**

Page 90
1. cap
2. cup
3. cat
4. cut
5. bug
6. bag
7. fan
8. fun

Page 91
short **e**:
desk, bet, nest, tent
short **u**:
hug, duck, tub, truck

Page 92
1. pig
2. bus
3. mittens
4. cup
5. fish
6. drum

Page 93
1. mop
2. duck
3. doll
4. bus
5. lock
6. fox

Page 94
1. e
2. i
3. o
4. u
5. a
6. e
7. i
8. e
9. i
10. u
11. a
12. i
13. u
14. a
15. o
16. i

Blends: fl

This is Flora's first day of school.
Can you help Flora with her blends?

Use the **fl** words in the box to finish the puzzle.

flower	fly	floor
flame	flute	flag

Across

1. an insect

2. we stand on it

3. it can make music

Down

1. a rose is one

2. light given off from fire

3. all countries have one

Blends: pl, sl

It is time for recess on the playground.

Write the **sl** words on the slide.
Write the **pl** words on the plane.

planet	plane	plate
sleep	plant	slip
sled	slam	
please	slice	

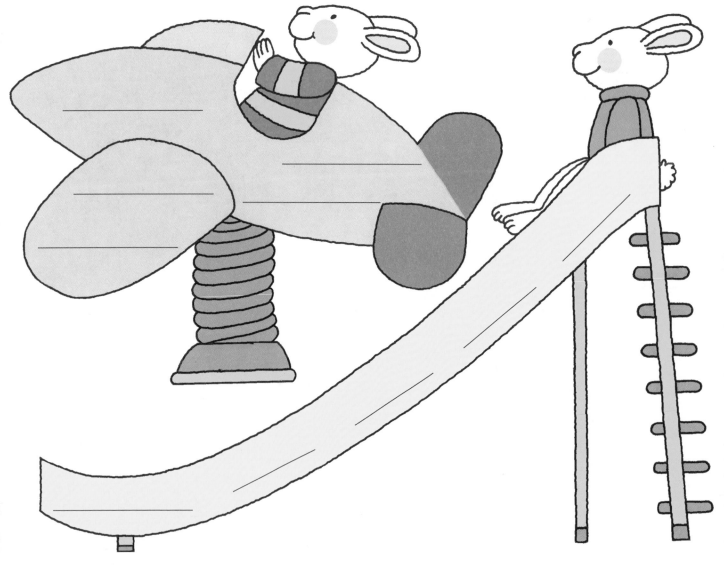

Blends: bl, cl, gl

Help the class do a blend puzzle.

Read each clue. Use the words in the box to finish the puzzle.

blue	clock	clean	glue
blocks	cloud	glad	glove
black	clothes	globe	

Across
2. opposite of white
4. holds things together
5. a form of moisture in the sky
7. building toys
9. a round map
10. opposite of dirty

Down
1. what we wear
3. it keeps time
4. happy
6. worn on the hand
8. color of the sky

REVIEW: Blends

Today, Glen came to our class. Learn more about Glen.

Underline the words that begin with the following blends:

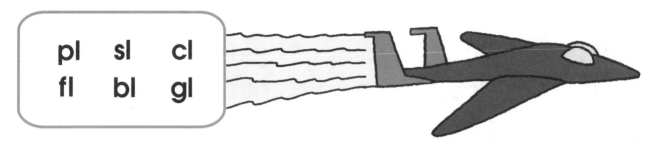

pl   sl   cl
fl   bl   gl

Glen is a pilot. His plane is silver and black. He flies

high in the clear, blue sky. Glen glides above the

clouds. He flies his plane around the globe. When

Glen sleeps, nobody knows.

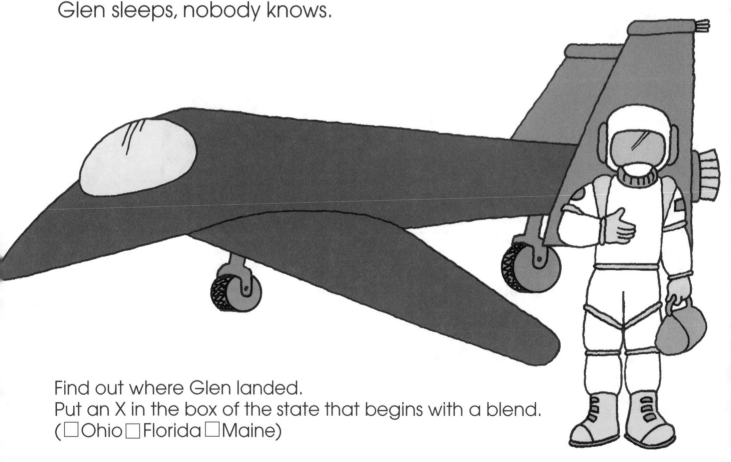

Find out where Glen landed.
Put an X in the box of the state that begins with a blend.
(□ Ohio □ Florida □ Maine)

                                                                 Review

Blends: br

Brent made a talking machine at school.
It makes **br** words.

Find the words the machine made.
Write the **br** words on the blanks.

broom branch bike bananas
brother boy bacon bright
broken brave

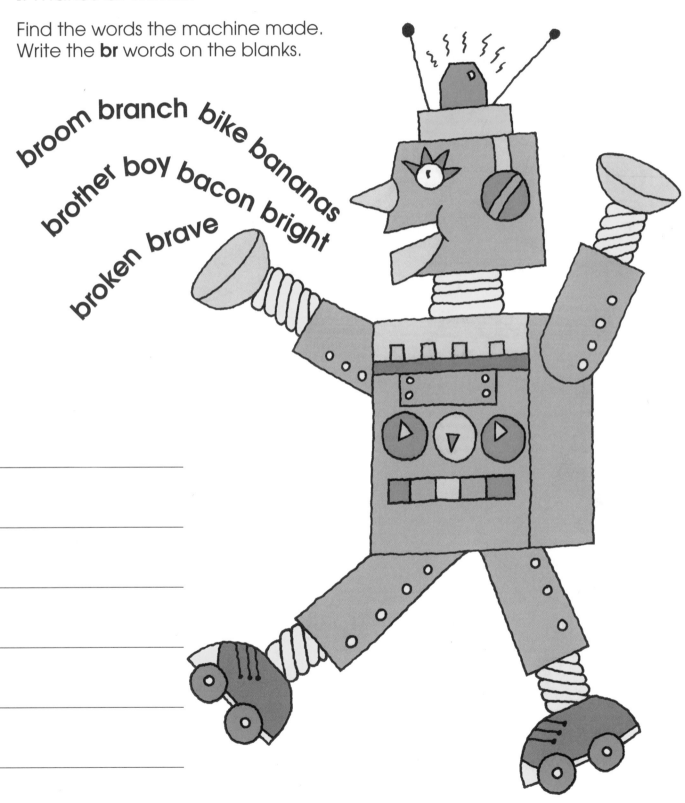

_____

_____

_____

_____

_____

Blends: cr

Chris is in art class. He is coloring **cr** words.

Help Chris color the words red that begin with **cr**.

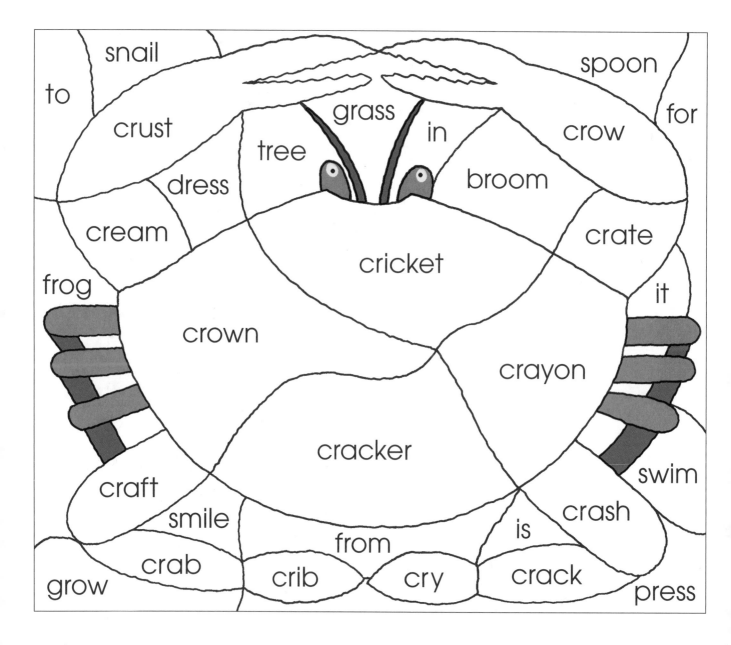

snail
to
crust
grass
in
spoon
for
crow
tree
dress
broom
cream
crate
frog
cricket
it
crown
crayon
cracker
craft
swim
smile
crash
crab
from
is
crack
grow
crib
cry
press

Chris colored a crazy _____ .

Blends: dr

Drinda has dreams of **dr** words.

Circle the words in her dream that begin with **dr**.

draw   drink   monkey

drum   clock
        lion

mine   nothing
        drip
    dragon

        driver

please   dress

    dark   dry

    zebra

Blends: fr

Fred is helping Frances learn **fr** words.

Write the correct **fr** word on the line to
answer the riddle.

frog	**front**
from	**fruit**
friend	**free**

1. Someone you like is a _____.

2. It is not the back. It is the _____.

3. Maria got a present _____ Jimmy.

4. A _____ is a green animal that hops.

5. Bananas are a _____ and so are apples.

6. We rode every ride because the tickets were _____.

Blends: gr

Greg had to write a paper about himself.
What did Greg write?

Write the missing **gr** words on the correct lines.

group	**grape**	**growl**	**grunt**
grass	**grow**	**green**	**Greg**

My name is _____. I like to play outside on the

_____ _____. Sometimes I pretend to

be a monster, and I _____ and _____.

I play monster with a _____ of friends.

Then Mom makes peanut butter and _____ jelly

sandwiches for us. Even monsters need food to _____!

Blends: tr

Trina is trying to trick Trent.
She made a **tr** crossword.

Write the missing letters to make **tr** words.
Find each word within the puzzle.

___ actor   ___ ee   ___ ick

___ ain   ___ y   ___ ip

___ uck   ___ ap   ___ ue

```
T R U C K T R Y
R R U E K T V R
A T R I P R T H
C R E C R I Y T
T R E E A C I R
O H T S A K P U
R U T R A P Y E
P W T R A I N I
```

Blends: tr

Travis is in study hall. Help Travis with his homework.

Finish the puzzle with a rhyming word.

true   trap   truck
tree   trip   trick

Across

2. slip

3. luck

4. bee

Down

1. clap

2. stick

3. blue

Blends: pr

Priscilla has a birthday party today.
Find out what the class will give her.

Write the **pr** blend on the blanks to make words.
Then connect the dots.

1. __ __ **etty** •

2. __ __ **ess** •

3. __ __ **esent** •

• 6. __ __ **ize**

• 5. __ __ **ince**

• 4. __ __ **oud**

Priscilla's classmates will give her a _____ .

REVIEW: Blends

It is Fun Day at recess. The students are on a treasure hunt.

Write the correct blend to finish each word. What will they find?

br   **cr**   **dr**   **fr**   **gr**   **pr**   **tr**

__ __ **ize**

__ __ **agon**

__ __ **apes**

__ __ **ead**

__ __ **og**

__ __ **ow**

__ __ **ee**

START →

Review

Blends: sm, sn

Sam's snail is on his way to school.
Help Sam follow his trail.

Write the **sm** or **sn** blend to finish the word.

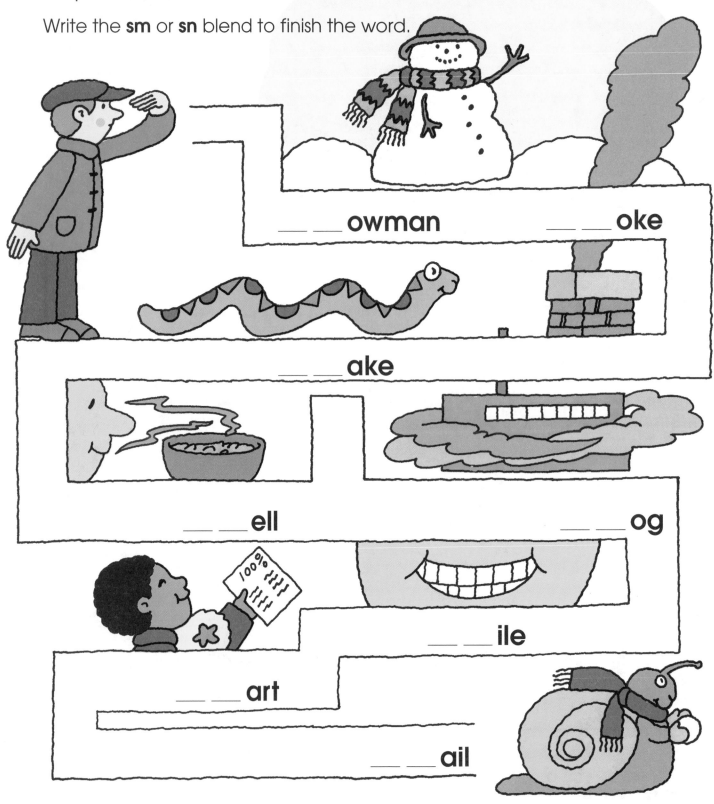

___ ___ **owman**

___ ___ **oke**

___ ___ **ake**

___ ___ **ell**

___ ___ **og**

___ ___ **ile**

___ ___ **art**

___ ___ **ail**

Blends: sw, sp

Swain and Spencer are at a swim meet.
Help them stay in their lanes.

Write the **sw** or **sp** blend to finish the word.

1. __ __ **im**

2. __ __ **an**

3. __ __ **ing**

4. __ __ **eet**

5. __ __ **ider**

6. __ __ **oon**

7. __ __ **ot**

8. __ __ **ring**

The class is taking a trip. Help them find the zoo.

Draw a line to connect all the **st** words.
The words may begin or end with **st**.

start sat crow

most stick bus

blue dust stack

bath shoe

path

bee

dish

shell

fox

store

best

last

just

stir

snap

food

boy

sun

ZOO

Blends: str, spr

It is show and tell time at school. What will Jill tell?

Write the correct **str** or **spr** words on the lines to finish the story.

street	**strawberry**	**spray**
stream	**sprinkler**	**spring**

Dad had to water the new ___ ___ ___ ___ ___ ___ ___ ___ ___ ___

plants. He put the ___ ___ ___ ___ ___ ___ ___ ___ ___ by the plants.

Then he turned on the water. A big ___ ___ ___ ___ ___ of water

shot into the air. It began to make a long ___ ___ ___ ___ ___ ___

down the ___ ___ ___ ___ ___ ___. Dad had to fix a bad

___ ___ ___ ___ ___ ___. Now we have lots of juicy berries to share.

REVIEW: Blends

Take a test with the class. Fill in the blanks with **s** blends to make words.

Name: _____

1. **str**   **sl**

    ___ ___ ___ awberry

2. **sl**   **sn**

    ___ ___ ail

3. **sm**   **st**

    ___ ___ amp

4. **spr**   **str**

    ___ ___ ___ inkler

5. **str**   **sw**

    ___ ___ ___ eam

6. **sl**   **sm**

    ___ ___ ile

7. **sw**   **st**

    ___ ___ im

8. **sl**   **st**

    ___ ___ ar

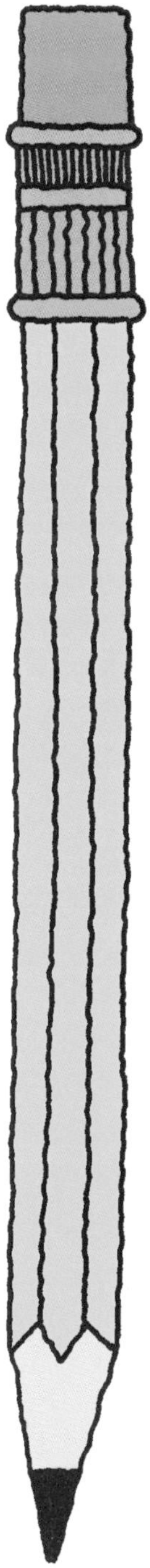

Combination Sounds: ch

Chad and Mitch have a **ch** project.
They need objects with the **ch** sound.

Draw a line from each word that **starts** with **ch** to Chad.
Draw a line from each word that **ends** with **ch** to Mitch.

cheese

porch

cow

dog

chair

banana

smile

watch

fish

bird

chimney

bear

catch

match

book

glass

cherry

man

Combination Sounds: sh

The class took an **sh** field trip.
They went to a sheep farm and a fish farm.

Write all the words that start with **sh** in the sheep pen.
Write all the words that end in **sh** in the fish pond.

push	shop	shoe
show	dish	shirt
shell	wash	wish

1. _____

2. _____

3. _____

4. _____

5. _____

6. _____

7. _____

8. _____

9. _____

Combination Sounds: **sh**

Combination Sounds: th

Help Thelma and Meredith write a paper.

Finish each sentence with the correct **th** word.

bath	**path**
there	**Thank**
thirty	**think**

Our dog, Rex, would not let us give him a _____ .

We _____ he's afraid of water. Rex tried to run from us, but

we followed his _____ . It took us almost _____

minutes to catch him. _____ goodness Mom was

_____ to help us!

Combination Sounds: wh

Mrs. White wants the class to learn how to whistle.
Help them whistle to all the **wh** words.

Write the missing letters to make **wh** words.
Find each word within the puzzle.

___ eel   ___ y   ___ en

___ eat   ___ ale   ___ at

___ istle   ___ ite   ___ ere

```
W H I S T L E
H H A W H Y W
A R W H A T H
L N X I T W E
E W H T T H R
W H E E L E E
W H E A T N S
```

REVIEW: Blends

It is time for lunch. What is on the menu?

Write the missing letters on the blanks.

ch th
sh wh

LUNCH MENU
Today's
SPECIAL

__ __ite milk

__ __eat bread

__ __icken sandwi__ __

bro __ __

__ __erry pie

soft __ __ell tacos

REVIEW: Blends

The children have their mittens mixed up.

Draw lines to show which mittens go together.

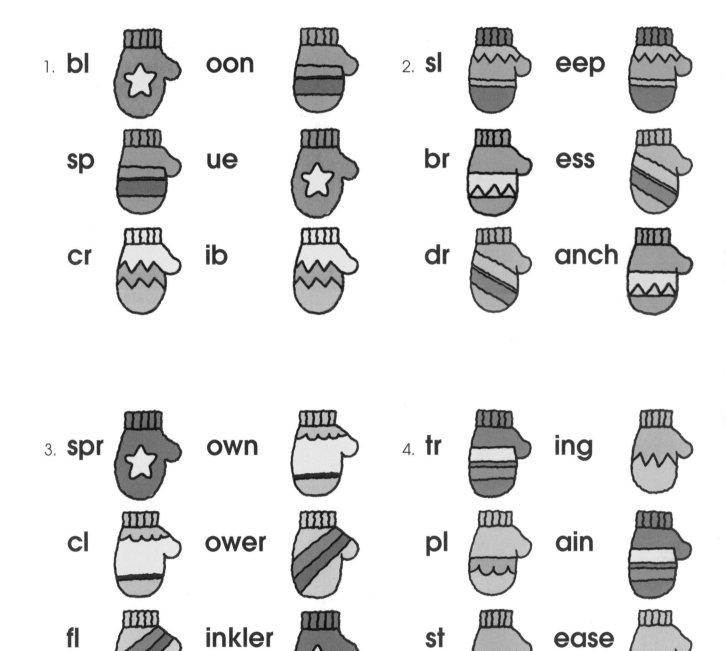

1. bl   oon

   sp   ue

   cr   ib

2. sl   eep

   br   ess

   dr   anch

3. spr   own

   cl   ower

   fl   inkler

4. tr   ing

   pl   ain

   st   ease

Review

REVIEW: Blends

Clara forgot to finish the blend words.

Write the missing letters to make a word.

ue	ee	ib	ock	ink
ag	og	ot	ove	owman

1. **bl** __ __

2. **fr** __ __

3. **sp** __ __

4. **tr** __ __

5. **gl** __ __ __

6. **fl** __ __

7. **cl** __ __ __

8. **cr** __ __

9. **dr** __ __ __

10. **sn** __ __ __ __ __

Review

REVIEW: Blends

Help the class learn about snails.

Underline each word that begins with the sounds in the box.

sn	sl	cr	pl
st	sh	gr	

A snail has a soft body covered by a shell. It creeps along on a foot. Its body has a head with feelers, eyes, a mouth, and tiny teeth. Land snails live in shady places. They lay eggs in the ground. A moving snail makes a sticky slime to help it move. Snails live almost everywhere.

REVIEW: Blends

Brent has homework to do.
Help Brent finish the puzzle.

Jack	click	brown
crack	black	clown

Across

2. opposite of white

3. a funny person

4. a break

Down

1. a name

2. a color

3. a sound

REVIEW: Blends

School is over for the year.
What does Shelly find in her desk?

Draw a line from each picture to the
sound you hear in each word.

ch   sh   th   wh

REVIEW: Blends

It is summer vacation. Keep your skills sharp.

Write the missing letters to make words that end with **ch**, **sh**, and **th** sounds. Then find each word in the puzzle.

mat___   wa___   mou___

chur___   pu___   sou___

wat___   di___   pa___

por___   ba___

```
W P A T H W D M
B O H S J A I O
A R I O K T S U
T C H U R C H T
H H M T T H L H
P U S H W A S H
M A T C H W E L
```

Review

Answer Key

Page 97

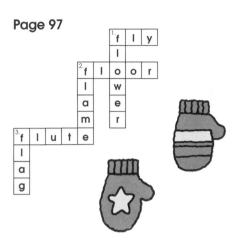

1. fly
2. floor
3. flute
   - flower
   - flame
   - flag

Page 98

pl words:
plant, planet, plate, please, plane

sl words:
sleep, sled, slice, slam, slip

Page 99

1. cloth
2. black
3. clock
4. glue
5. cloud
6. glove
7. blocks
8. blue
9. globe
10. clean
- glad

Page 100

Glen, plane, black, flies, clear, blue, Glen, glides, clouds, flies, plane, globe, Glen, sleeps
(Florida)

Page 101

brother, broom, broken, bright, brave, branch

Page 102

crust, cream, crown, cricket, cracker, crayon, crate, crow, craft, crab, crib, cry, crack, crash
(crab)

Page 103

draw, drink, drum, dragon, dress, drip, dry, driver

Page 104

1. friend
2. front
3. from
4. frog
5. fruit
6. free

Page 105

Greg, green, grass, grunt, growl, group, grape, grow

Page 106

```
T R U C K T R Y
R R U E K T V R
A T R I P R T H
C R E C R I Y T
T R E E A C I R
O H T S A K P U
R U T R A P Y E
P W T R A I N I
```

Page 107

1. tra
2. trip
3. truck
4. tree
   - trick
   - truce

Page 108

1. pretty
2. press
3. present
4. proud
5. prince
6. prize
(present)

Page 109

crow, tree, frog, bread, dragon, grapes, prize

Page 110

snowman, smoke, snake, smell, smog, smile, smart, snail

Page 111

1. swim
2. swan
3. swing
4. sweet
5. spider
6. spoon
7. spot
8. spring

Answer Key

Pages 112-113
start, most, stick, dust, stack, just, stir, store, best, last

Page 114
strawberry, sprinkler, spray, stream, street, spring

Page 115
1. strawberry 2. snail
3. stamp   4. sprinkler
5. stream   6. smile
7. swim   8. star

Page 116
Chad
chimney, cheese, cherry, chair

Mitch
porch, watch, match, catch

Page 117
1. shell   6. dish
2. show   7. push
3. shoe   8. wish
4. shirt   9. wash
5. shop

Page 118
bath, think, path, thirty, Thank, there

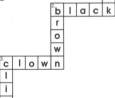

Page 119

```
W H I S T L E
H H A W H Y W
A R W H A T H
L N X I T W E
E W H T V H R
W H E E L E E
W H E A T N S
```

Page 120
white milk
wheat bread
chicken sandwich
broth
cherry pie
soft shell tacos

Page 121
1. blue   2. sleep
   spoon   branch
   crib   dress

3. sprinkler 4. train
   clown   please
   flower   sting

Page 122
All words are acceptable answers.

Page 123
snail, shell, creeps, snails, shady, places, ground, snail, sticky, slime, Snails

Page 124

```
          J
          a
    b l a c k
    r
    o
  c l o w n
  l
  i
  c
c r a c k
```

Page 125
ch
cherry, cheese, watch
sh
shirt, sheep, dish, shoe
th
bath, three
wh
whale, wheel, whistle

Page 126
```
W P A T H W D M
B O H S J A I O
A R I O K T S U
T C H U R C H T
H H M T T H L H
P U S H W A S H
M A T C H W E L
```

Beginning Consonants

Write the missing letter for each animal name.
Say the word.

1. __ear

2. __at

3. __og

4. __ish

5. __oat

6. __orse

7. __aguar

8. __angaroo

9. __ion

10. __ouse

11. __ightingale

12. __ig

13. __uail

14. __abbit

15. __eal

16. __iger

17. __ulture

18. __alrus

19. __ak

20. __ebra

Short Vowel Sounds: a

Read the short **a** words in the box.
Then do what each sentence tells you.

at	as	cat
fan	am	ant
an	had	

1. Write the words that have two letters.

_____ _____ _____ _____

2. Write the words that have three letters.

_____ _____ _____ _____

Make short **a** words.
Write the short **a** endings.
Say the word.

at	**am**	**an**	**ad**
1. b____	5. h____	9. r____	13. b____
2. h____	6. j____	10. m____	14. d____
3. m____	7. S____	11. p____	15. h____
4. p____	8. r____	12. f____	16. m____

Short Vowel Sounds: e

Answer the riddles. Use the words in the box below.
Write the word on the line.

tent	**nest**	**bed**	**desk**
ten	**cent**	**belt**	**hen**
bell	**pen**	**red**	**sled**

1. We can ride on it in winter. _____

2. We write with it. _____

3. We can sleep in it outdoors. _____

4. It makes a ringing sound. _____

5. Firetrucks are often this color. _____

6. A dime is this many pennies. _____

7. It lays eggs. _____

8. We sit at one in school. _____

9. It holds up your pants. _____

10. We sleep on it. _____

11. A penny is one. _____

12. Baby birds stay in it. _____

Short Vowel Sounds: i

Write the short vowel **i** in the blanks to complete the silly sentences.
Read the sentences to a friend.

1. I h __ d the l __ d, I d __ d.

2. I w __ ll f __ ll the h __ ll with flowers.

3. I w __ sh the f __ sh were still in the d __ sh.

4. The b __ g p __ g ate a f __ g.

Add the beginning letter to make short **i** words from the sentences above.

1. __ id   2. __ ill   3. __ ish   4. __ ig

__ id   __ ill   __ ish   __ ig

__ id   __ ill   __ ish   __ ig

Write two silly sentences with a short **i** word.

_____

_____

Short Vowel Sounds: o

Add an **o** to the letters to make short **o** words.

hot **hop** **rock**

1. n __ t   3. t __ p   5. s __ ck

2. p __ t   4. m __ p   6. l __ ck

Finish the sentence with a short **o** word.

got	top	job	doll
lot	box	hot	sock

1. Put the toys back in the _____ .

2. I cannot find my other _____ .

3. My sister _____ a bike for her birthday.

4. Be careful! The soup is _____ .

5. Zach's father has a new _____ .

6. There is snow on _____ of the mountain.

7. Mother made a new dress for my _____ .

8. There are a _____ of leaves to rake.

Short Vowel Sounds: u

Read the short **u** words in the umbrella.
Write two pairs of words that have the same ending.

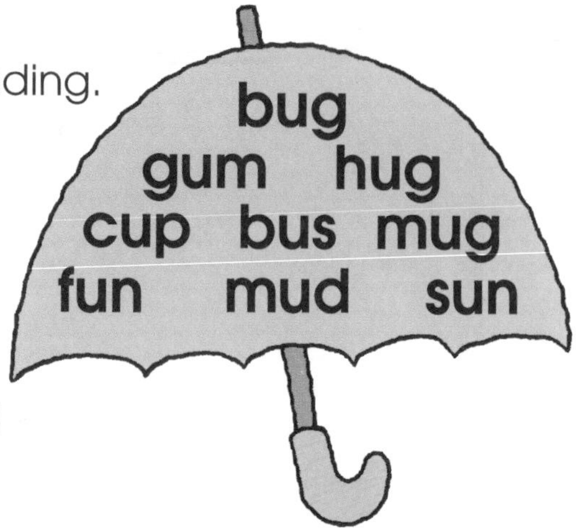

1. _____ 2. _____

_____ _____

bug
gum hug
cup bus mug
fun mud sun

Write the beginning letter of each picture word
to make a word. The first one is done for you.

1.  🍳 + ☂ + 🍳 p u p

2.  🐐 + ☂ + 🌙 _ _ _

3.  🌀 + ☂ + 🥮 _ _ _

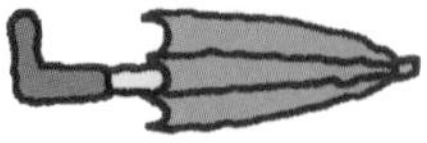

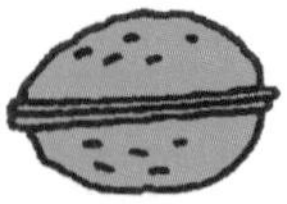

4.  🎩 + ☂ + 🐐 _ _ _

5.  ⚽ + ☂ + 🐐 _ _ _

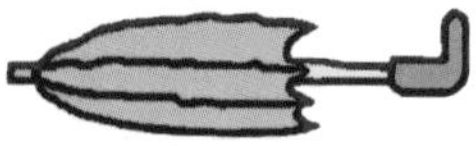

6.  🐱 + ☂ + 🍳 _ _ _

7.  ✂ + ☂ + 🥮 _ _ _

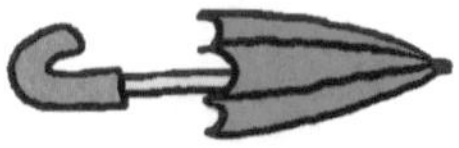

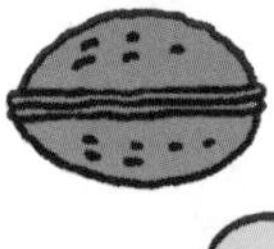

8.  🌙 + ☂ + 🐕 _ _ _

REVIEW: Short Vowels

Add the correct short vowel to finish each word in the picture.
Each picture word has the same vowel sound.
Write the words on the lines under the correct vowel.

c _ t

m _ n

h _ n

r _ d

s _ n

b _ s

t _ p

h _ p

p _ g

b _ g

a

1. _____

_____

e

2. _____

_____

i

3. _____

_____

o

4. _____

_____

u

5. _____

_____

Short Vowel Review

Long Vowel Sounds: a

The letters **ay** and **ai** make the long **a** sound.

Silly Snail is on the trail to get her pail.
What did she see on the way?
Write the name of each long **a** object
on the blanks. Use the words in the box.

jay   mail   train
tray   rain   paint
pail   hay   chain

Silent e

Add **e** to the word to make a long vowel word.
Then say the word.

1. can __ 2. tub __ 3. pin __ 4. rob __ 5. plan __

6. cub __ 7. dim __ 8. not __ 9. rid __ 10. sam __

11. cut __ 12. cap __ 13. kit __ 14. tim __ 15. tap __

Write the **bold** word from each sentence on the line.
Then add an **e**.
Read the sentence.

1. She **can** walk with a _____ .

2. The light was so **dim** I lost my _____ .

3. Dad did not **plan** to go by _____ .

4. I bought a **kit** to make a _____ .

5. **Sam** looks the _____ as he did last year.

Silent **e**

Long Vowel Sounds: e

Long **e** sounds are made by **ea**, **ee**, or **ey**.

Write the words to finish the puzzle.

dream	bean	key
clean	leave	seed
money	tree	see

Across

2. produces a plant

5. go away

7. used to buy things

8. a kind of vegetable

Down

1. a large plant

2. look at

3. it happens when asleep

4. the opposite of dirty

6. opens locks

Long Vowel Sounds: i

The letters **y, igh**, and sometimes **ie** have the long **i** sound.

Color the long **i** words red. Color the words that are not long **i** blue.

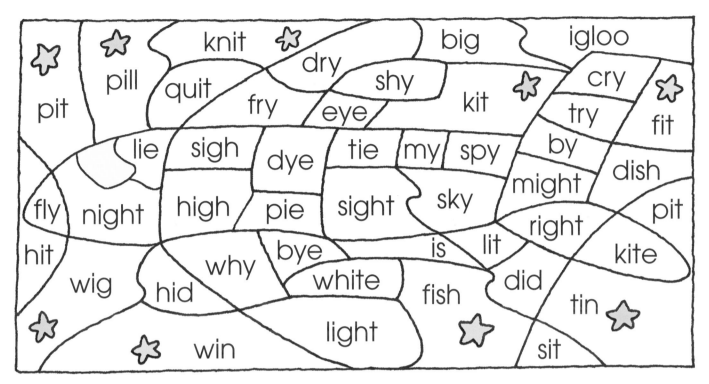

Write the long **i** words from above to complete the story.

It is **n** __ __ __ **t**. There is no **l** __ __ __ **t** in the **sk** __. We heard a

plane **fl** __ **b** __ **h** __ __ __ above us. Seth let out a **s** __ __ __.

"Someday," he said, "I will **tr** __ to learn how to **fl** __.

But **r** __ __ __ **t** now, let's go have a piece of Mom's **p** __ __ !"

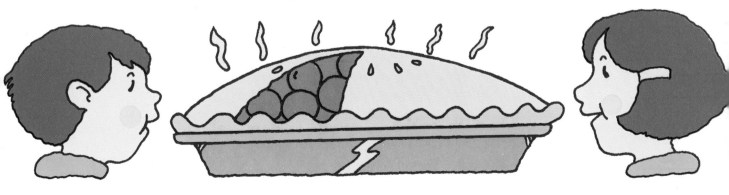

Long Vowel Sounds: o

The letters **oa** and **ow** usually make the long **o** sound.

Write the words to finish the puzzle.

snow	goat	toast	road
show	low	slow	grow

Across

2. another name for a movie

3. get bigger

4. browned bread

6. a highway

Down

1. opposite of high

2. frozen rain

3. a farm animal with horns

5. opposite of fast

Long Vowel Sounds: u

The letters **ew**, **u-e**, **ue**, and **ui** make the long **u** sound.

Use long **u** letter combinations to finish the words in each group.
Write the whole word on the line. Say the word.

ew

1. n___ _____

2. d___ _____

3. bl___ _____

ue

7. d___ _____

8. gl___ _____

9. bl___ _____

u-e

4. h__g__ _____

5. c__b__ _____

6. t__b__ _____

ui

10. fr___t _____

11. j___ce _____

12. s___t _____

REVIEW: Long Vowels

Write the words to finish the puzzle.

light   dime   honey   boat
new   rain   play   clean

Down

1. not heavy

3. food made by bees

5. free from dirt

8. never used

Across

2. equal to ten pennies

4. small ship

6. you do this to an instrument

7. drops of water from clouds

142

Blends: l

Common blends are: **bl**, **gl**, **cl**, **pl**, **fl**, and **sl**.

Write the **l** blends to make new words.
Say each word.
Find each blend word in the puzzle below.

1. **bl**

___ock

___ue

___ink

2. **gl**

___ad

___obe

___itter

3. **cl**

___own

___ock

___ub

4. **pl**

___an

___ay

___us

5. **fl**

___ower

___ag

___y

6. **sl**

___ip

___eep

___ow

```
B L I N K B L O C K G S G
P L U S S L I P L F L D L
C L U B W U R N O D A U O
N S K I C E N A W L D P B
F L A G S L O W N T S L E
L E O C P C L O C K E A G
Y E B G L I T T E R O Y T
T P L A N L F L O W E R F
```

143

Blends: s

Write the **s** blends to make new words. Say each word.
Complete the story below with **s** blend words.

1. **sk** _ _ in
   _ _ ip

2. **sh** _ _ ape
   _ _ ell

3. **sp** _ _ eed
   _ _ ill

4. **st** _ _ ory
   _ _ amp

5. **sl** _ _ eep
   _ _ ime

6. **sn** _ _ ap
   _ _ ail

7. **sm** _ _ oke
   _ _ all

8. **sw** _ _ eet
   _ _ im

This is a **st** _ _ _ of a **sm** _ _ _ _   **sn** _ _ _ named **Sk** _ _ .

Sk _ _ lives in a curly **sh** _ _ _ . His **sk** _ _ feels

like **sl** _ _ _ . **Sp** _ _ _ does not matter to him. If he is in

danger, he goes into his **sh** _ _ _ . He also goes into his

sh _ _ _ to **sl** _ _ _ . **Sw** _ _ _ dreams, **Sk** _ _ !

Blends: r

Color the **r** blends green to make a picture.
Choose a blend word to fill the blanks below.

br   **pr**   **dr**   **tr**

  fr   **gr**   **cr**

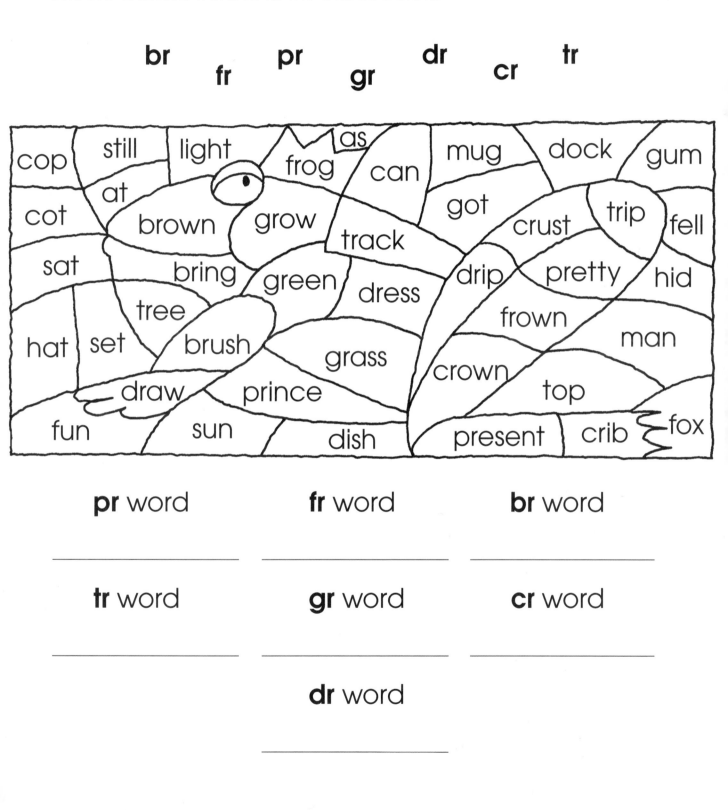

pr word   **fr** word   **br** word

_____   _____   _____

tr word   **gr** word   **cr** word

_____   _____   _____

                           dr word

                      _____

REVIEW: Blends

Make blend words by adding the **bold** ending.
Say each word.
The first one is done for you.

1. gr**ay**   M a y   tr___   pl___
2. cr**y**   fr__   fl__   sk__
3. dr**ip**   fl___   sl___   sk___
4. gr**ow**   bl___   cr___   sl___
5. br**own**   dr____   fr____   cl____
6. sk**ill**   sp____   st____   gr____
7. cr**ack**   tr____   bl____   st____
8. br**ing**   cl____   fl____   st____

Blends Review

Combination Sounds

Some letters make a new sound when they are put together.

shell	cherry	third	think
wheel	whale	ship	chair

Write the words from the box above that **begin** like the following words:

1. **ch**ild _____ _____

2. **th**ick _____ _____

3. **wh**ite _____ _____

4. **sh**op _____ _____

north	watch	fish

Write the words from the box above that **end** like the following words:

5. ea**ch** _____

6. ba**th** _____

7. wa**sh** _____

Same Sounds: oi, oy

The letters **oi** and **oy** have the same sound.

Find each word in the puzzle below.

boil	**joy**	**point**	**broil**
oil	**toy**	**soil**	**moist**
join	**boy**	**coin**	**voice**

```
B N S O I L L C O R T
R T U E S J O Y L F O
O L N B P E I N B O Y
I L A B O I L K N T S
L S V R I S T J W L F
L E O C N L C O I N O
M O I S T I U I E R I
T P C A N L F N O W S
W E E O K T P G A V E
```

Write a sentence using an **oi** word.

_____

Write a sentence using an **oy** word.

_____

Letter Combinations: oo, ue, ew

Answer the riddles. Use the words in the box below.
Write the word on the line.

moose	blue	tooth	pool
school	true	stool	dew
broom	glue	chew	new

1. It is the color of the sky. _____

2. You can find this on the grass in the morning. _____

3. Things stick together with it. _____

4. It is a big animal with antlers. _____

5. It is the opposite of old. _____

6. This is what you do with gum. _____

7. You can sit on it. _____

8. You can sweep the floor with it. _____

9. It is the opposite of false. _____

10. You should brush it twice a day. _____

11. This is where you go to learn. _____

12. You go swimming in this. _____

Letter Combinations: **oo, ue, ew**

Letter Combinations: ou, ow

Answer the riddles. Use the words in the box below.
Write the word on the line.

brown   crown   sour
hound   mouse   out
clown   howl

1. A lemon is this. _____

2. Tree trunks are this color. _____

3. A king wears one. _____

4. This word means the opposite of in. _____

5. A hunting dog is sometimes called this. _____

6. This is a funny person in a circus. _____

7. Wolves make this sound. _____

8. It is a rodent with small ears and a long tail. _____

Write two sentences. Use an **ow** word in one sentence
and an **ou** word in the other.

_____

_____

Silent Letters

Sometimes the letters **l**, **k**, **w**, **h**, **t**, **b**, and **gh** are silent.

Add the silent letters.
Then say the word.

1. **w**

___rap

___rong

___rite

2. **gh**

hi___ ___

si___ ___

ni___ ___t

3. **b**

dum___

thum___

crum___

4. **t**

ca___ch

ma___ch

swi___ch

5. **k**

___nob

___nit

___nee

6. **l**

wa___k

sta___k

ta___k

7. **h**

___onest

___our

g___ost

See if you can finish each word.

8. ri___ ___t

9. lam___

10. ca___f

11. ___rite

12. la___ch

13. ___nock

14. ___onor

15. bri___ ___t

16. ki___chen

Same Sounds: ir, er, ur

The letter combinations **ir**, **er**, and **ur** have the same **r** sound.

Write the words to finish the puzzle.

farmer	bird	purse
father	girl	shirt
dinner	nurse	turtle

Across

2. a person who works on a farm

5. a sister is one

6. a feathered animal

7. a cloth garment with collar and sleeves

8. used to carry money and small objects

Down

1. a person who cares for the sick

2. the male parent

3. a reptile with a shell

4. one of three daily meals

Different Sounds: c, g

Copy the words. Say each word.

The letter **c** sounds like **k** before these vowels: **a o u**.

The letter **c** sounds like **s** before these vowels: **i e**.

1. cat _____
2. cow _____
3. cake _____
4. cup _____

5. city _____
6. circus _____
7. cent _____
8. circle _____

The letter **g** sounds like the **g** in goat before these vowels: **a o u**.

The letter **g** usually sounds like **j** before these vowels: **i e**.

9. gas _____
10. gum _____
11. good _____
12. got _____

13. general _____
14. gem _____
15. gentle _____
16. giraffe _____

Different Sounds: **c, g**

Contractions

When you use an apostrophe to put words together, you form a contraction.

Choose the correct contraction to finish the sentence.

aren't	**I'll**	**they'll**
don't	**isn't**	**they're**
can't	**We're**	**couldn't**

1. The socks _____ match.

do not

2. I _____ read her writing.

could not

3. _____ going on vacation tomorrow.

We are

4. Hanna _____ home.

is not

5. _____ bake cookies tonight.

I will

6. Why _____ the dogs in the pen?

are not

7. I was told _____ on the way home.

they are

8. Seth _____ find his baseball.

cannot

9. Our grandparents said _____ see us Saturday.

they will

Compound Words

Make one word out of two!

Look at the pictures.
Then write the compound word on the line.
The first one is done for you.

1. _football_

2. _____

3. _____

4. _____

5. _____

6. _____

7. _____

Plural Endings

Plural means more than one. Here are some different ways to make a word plural. Sometimes you add **s**. Write the word, adding **s**.

1. book _____
2. hand _____
3. doll _____

4. clock _____
5. flower _____
6. mother _____

When the word ends in **x**, **ss**, **ch**, or **sh**, you add **es**.

7. box _____
8. dress _____
9. wish _____

10. pitch _____
11. bench _____
12. dish _____

When the word ends in **y**, usually you change the **y** to **i** and add **es**.

13. baby _____
14. pony _____
15. city _____

16. cherry _____
17. berry _____
18. penny _____

When the word ends in **f**, you change the **f** to **v** and add **es**.

19. leaf _____
20. wife _____

21. knife _____
22. shelf _____

Plural Endings

Suffixes

Words can have different endings.

Read the directions for each group.
Write the word with the correct ending.
Say the word.

Add ing

1. think _____

2. sing _____

3. work _____

Add ness or less

4. sick _____

5. care _____

6. kind _____

7. help _____

Drop e and add ing

8. save _____

9. make _____

10. come _____

Double the last letter and add ing

11. run _____

12. swim _____

13. jog _____

Add er or est

14. fast _____

15. slow _____

16. old _____

17. hard _____

Add ful

18. care _____

19. thank _____

20. help _____

Prefixes: un, mis

Un in front of a word means **not**.
Finish the word puzzle using the prefix **un**.

1. not happy

u	n	h	a	p	p	y

2. not able

3. not safe

4. not kind

5. not even

6. not tied

Mis in front of a word means **wrong**.
Finish the word puzzle using the prefix **mis**.

7. wrong fit

8. wrong place

9. wrong deal

10. wrong fire

11. wrong count

12. wrong spell

Answer Key

Page 129
1. bear
2. cat
3. dog
4. fish
5. goat
6. horse
7. jaguar
8. kangaroo
9. lion
10. mouse
11. nightingale
12. pig
13. quail
14. rabbit
15. seal
16. tiger
17. vulture
18. walrus
19. yak
20. zebra

Page 130
1. at, an, am, as
2. cat, ant, had, fan

1. bat
2. hat
3. mat
4. pat
5. ham
6. jam
7. Sam
8. ram
9. ran
10. man
11. pan
12. fan
13. bad
14. dad
15. had
16. mad

Page 131
1. sled
2. pen
3. tent
4. bell
5. red
6. ten
7. hen
8. desk
9. belt
10. bed
11. cent
12. nest

Page 132
1. hid, lid, did
2. will, fill, hill
3. wish, fish, dish
4. big, pig, fig

Answers will vary.

Page 133
1. not
2. pot
3. top
4. mop
5. sock
6. lock

1. box
2. sock
3. got
4. hot
5. job
6. top
7. doll
8. lot

Page 134
1. bug/mug/hug
2. sun/fun

1. **pup**
2. gum
3. fun
4. hug
5. bug
6. cup
7. sun
8. mud

Page 135
1. cat
   man
2. hen
   red
3. pig
   big
4. top
   hop
5. sun
   bus

Page 136
paint, chain,
hay, rain, train,
mail, tray, jay, pail

Page 137
1. cane
2. tube
3. pine
4. robe
5. plane
6. cube
7. dime
8. note
9. ride
10. same
11. cute
12. cape
13. kite
14. time
15. tape

1. cane
2. dime
3. plane
4. kite
5. same

Page 138

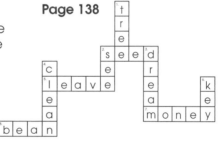

Crossword:
- t
- r
- e
- seed
- c
- e
- r
- k
- leave
- e
- e
- e
- l
- a
- a
- y
- e
- money
- bean

Page 139
night, light, sky
fly, by, high, sigh
try, fly
right, pie

Page 140

Crossword:
- l
- o
- show
- n
- o
- grow
- o
- a
- toast
- road
- w

Page 141
1. new
2. dew
3. blew
4. huge
5. cube
6. tube

7. due
8. glue
9. blue
10. fruit
11. juice
12. suit

Page 142

Crossword:
- l
- dime
- g
- h
- h
- boat
- n
- e
- c
- play
- e
- rain
- n
- e
- w

Page 143
1. block
   blue
   blink
2. glad
   globe
   glitter
3. clown
   clock
   club
4. plan
   play
   plus
5. flower
   flag
   fly
6. slip
   sleep
   slow

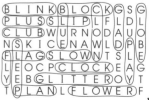

Word search:
BLINK BLOCK G S G
PLUS SLIP L F L D L
CLUB W U R N O D A U P
N S K I C E N A W L D P E
FLAG S L O W N T S L A E
L E O C P CLOCK E A G T
Y E B GLITTER O V T
T PLAN L FLOWER F

Answer Key

1. skin
   skip
2. shape
   shell
3. speed
   spill
4. story
   stamp
5. sleep
   slime
6. snap
   snail
7. smoke
   small
8. sweet
   swim

story, small, snail, Skip
Skip, shell, skin
slime, Speed
shell
shell, sleep, Sweet, Skip

Page 145
Automatic fill-in.

Page 146
1. May, tray, play
2. fry, fly, sky
3. flip, slip, skip
4. blow, crow, slow
5. drown, frown, clown
6. spill, still, grill
7. track, black, stack
8. cling, fling, sting

Page 147
1. cherry, chair
2. third, think
3. whale, wheel
4. shell, ship
5. watch
6. north
7. fish

Page 148

```
B N S O I L L C O R T
R T U E S J O Y L F O
O L N B P E I N B O Y
I L A B O I L K N T S
L S V R I S T J W L F
E O C N L C O I N O
M O I S T I U I E R I
T P C A N L F N O W S
W E E O K T P G A V E
```

Sentences will vary.

Page 149
1. blue
2. dew
3. glue
4. moose
5. new
6. chew
7. stool
8. broom
9. true
10. tooth
11. school
12. pool

Page 150
1. sour
2. brown
3. crown
4. out
5. hound
6. clown
7. howl
8. mouse

Sentences will vary.

Page 151
1. wrap
   wrong
   write
2. high
   sigh
   night
3. dumb
   thumb
   crumb
4. catch
   match
   switch
5. knob
   knit
   knee
6. walk
   stalk
   talk
7. honest
   hour
   ghost
8. right
9. lamb
10. calf
11. write
12. latch
13. knock
14. honor
15. bright
16. kitchen

Page 152
```
      ²f a r m e r    ⁴d
       a           ⁵g i r l
¹n     t           n
 u     h           n
 r  ⁷s h i r ³t  ⁸p u r s e
 s  e       u           e
 e          r
            t
            l
            e
```

Page 153
Automatic fill-in.

Page 154
1. don't
2. couldn't
3. We're
4. isn't
5. I'll
6. aren't
7. they're
8. can't
9. they'll

Page 155
1. **football**
2. birdhouse
3. rainbow
4. doorbell
5. starfish
6. watchdog
7. fireman

Page 156
1. books
2. hands
3. dolls
4. clocks
5. flowers
6. mothers

7. boxes
8. dresses
9. wishes
10. pitches
11. benches
12. dishes

13. babies
14. ponies
15. cities
16. cherries
17. berries
18. pennies

19. leaves
20. wives
21. knives
22. shelves

Page 157
1. thinking
2. singing
3. working
4. sickness
5. careless
6. kindness
7. helpless
8. saving
9. making
10. coming
11. running
12. swimming
13. jogging
14. faster, fastest
15. slower, slowest
16. older, oldest
17. harder, hardest
18. careful
19. thankful
20. helpful

Page 158
1. unhappy
2. unable
3. unsafe
4. unkind
5. uneven
6. untied
7. misfit
8. misplace
9. misdeal
10. misfire
11. miscount
12. misspell

Beginning Sounds

Say the word for each picture.
Write the **beginning** sound.
Use these letters: **c**, **f**, **h**, **k**, **m**, **p**, **r**, **t**.

1. ____ an

2. ____ ie

3. ____ ain

4. ____ ie

5. ____ at

6. ____ at

7. ____ ie

8. ____ an

____ ite

Beginning Sounds

Say the word for each picture.
Write the **beginning** sound.
Use these letters: **b, d, g, l, n, q, s, y**.

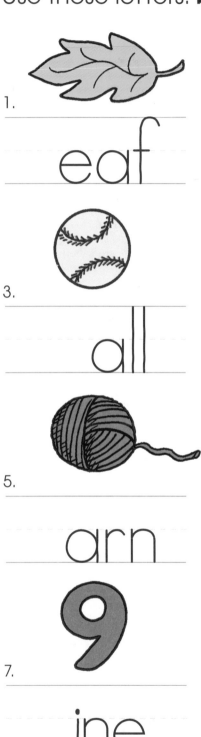

1. _____ eaf

3. _____ all

5. _____ arn

7. _____ ine

2. _____ og

4. _____ ueen

6. _____ oat

8. _____ oap

Ending Sounds

Say the word for each picture.
Write the **ending** sound.
Use these letters: **b**, **g**, **l**, **m**, **n**, **p**, **r**, **x**.

1.

pi _____

2.

su _____

3.

cu _____

4.

tu _____

5.

nai _____

6.

fo _____

7.

bea _____

8.

dru _____

Ending Sounds

Say the word for each picture.
Write the **ending** sound.
Use these letters: **d, f, k, l, o, s, t, r.**

1. be

2. sea

3. ca

4. e

5. o

zer

6. bu

7. ca

8. boo

Review

Say the word for each picture.
Write the **beginning** and **ending** sounds.
Use these letters: **m, n, p, s, g, t, b**.

1.
___ a ___

2.
___ o ___

3.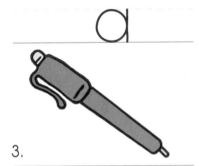
___ e ___

4.
___ u ___

5.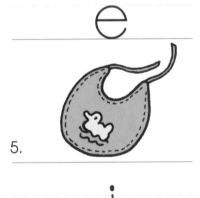
___ i ___

6.
___ a ___

7.
___ u ___

8.
___ e ___

Words with Short a

These words have the short **a** sound in .
Say the words.

pan   map   fan
nap   dad   bat

Write two words that **rhyme** with each picture.

1. _____

_____

_____

2. _____

_____

_____

Write the word that **begins** with the same letter as each picture.

1. _____

_____

2. _____

_____

Words with Short a

Write the short **a** words.
Then color the short **a** words in the picture blue.

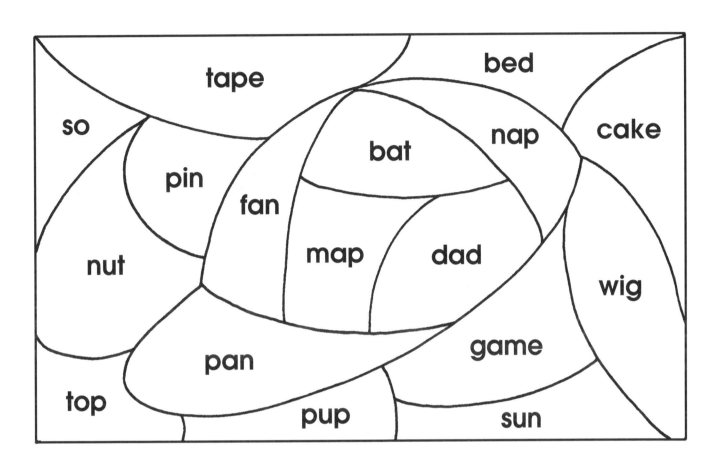

_____   _____

_____   _____

_____   _____

_____   _____

_____   _____

_____   _____

Words with Short e

These words have the short **e** sound in .
Say the words.

pen	ten	bell
net	pet	bed

Write the word that fits each shape.

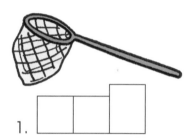

1. ▢▢▢

2. ▢▢

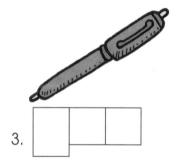

3. ▢▢▢

4. ▢▢▢

Write the word for each picture.

1. _____

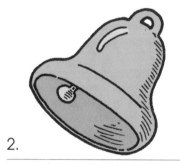

2. _____

Words with Short e

Write the short **e** words.
Then color the short **e** words in the picture red.

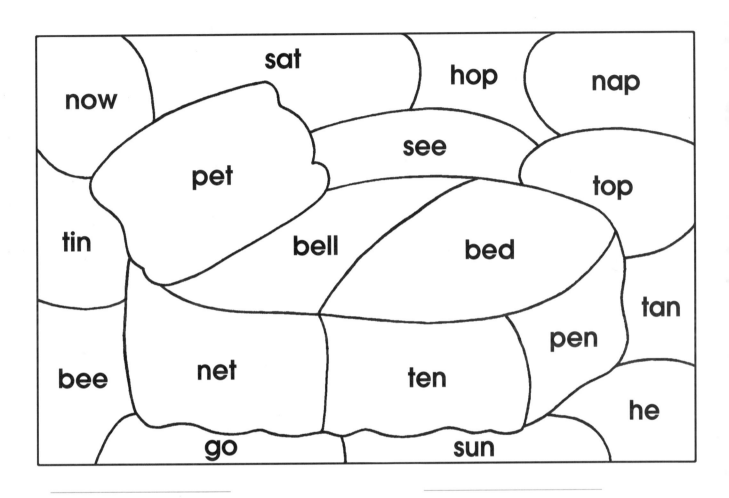

_____   _____

_____   _____

_____   _____

_____   _____

Words with Short i

These words have the short **i** sound in 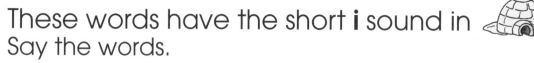 .
Say the words.

big	**dig**	**in**
pig	**wig**	**his**

Write a word that means the **opposite** of:

1.    out   _____

2.    hers

Write the words **ending** with **-ig**.

_____   _____

_____   _____

Words with Short i

Write the short **i** words.
Then color the short **i** words in the picture pink.

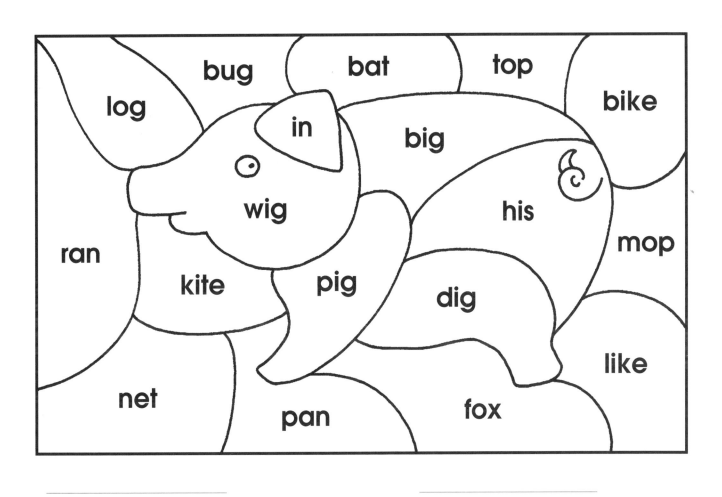

_____   _____

_____   _____

_____   _____

_____   _____

Words with Short o

These words have the short **o** sound in .
Say the words.

top	**box**	**sock**
pot	**not**	**lot**

Write the word for each picture inside the shape.

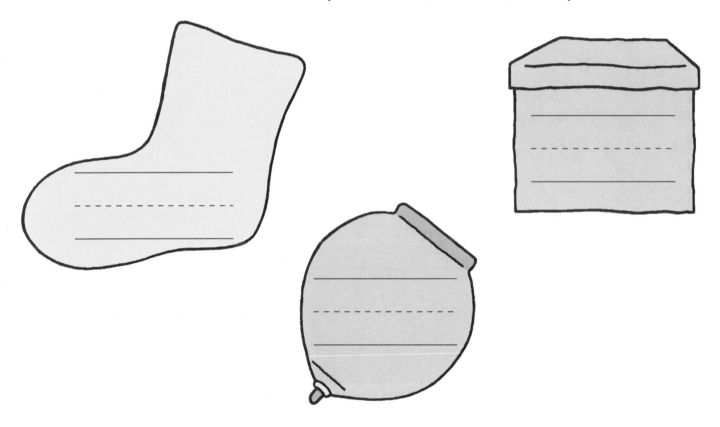

Write the words that **rhyme** with **hot**.

_____   _____   _____

_____   _____   _____

 Words with Short **o**

Words with Short o

Write the short **o** words.
Then color the short **o** words in the picture orange.

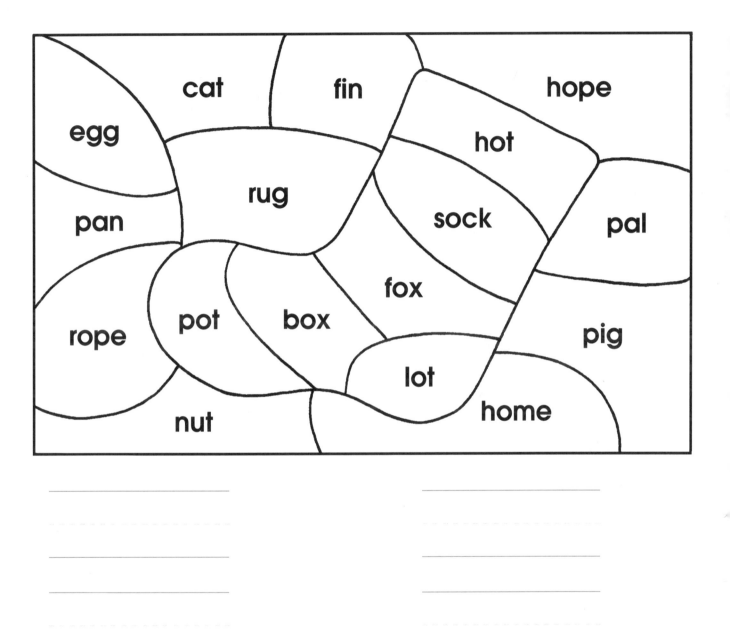

_____   _____

_____   _____

_____   _____

_____   _____

_____   _____

Words with Short u

These words have the short **u** sound in .
Say the words.

sun   rug   us
hug   up   run

Write a word that means the opposite of:

1.   down   _____

2.   moon      _____

3.   walk      _____

Write another word that begins with the same letter as each picture.

1. _____

2. _____

3. _____

Words with Short u

Write the short **u** word for each picture.
Say the words.

up	sun	rug
run	hug	bus

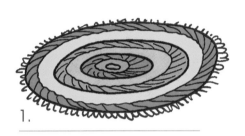

1. _____

2. _____

3. _____

4. _____

5. _____

6. _____

175

Review

Say the word for each picture.
Write the vowel.
Use these letters: **a, e, i, o, u**.

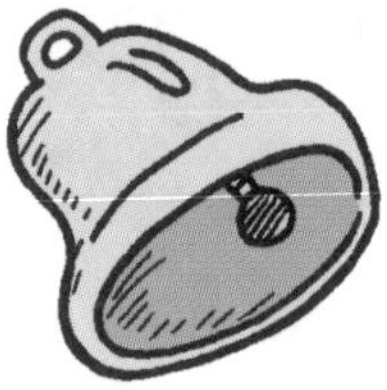

1. b __ l l

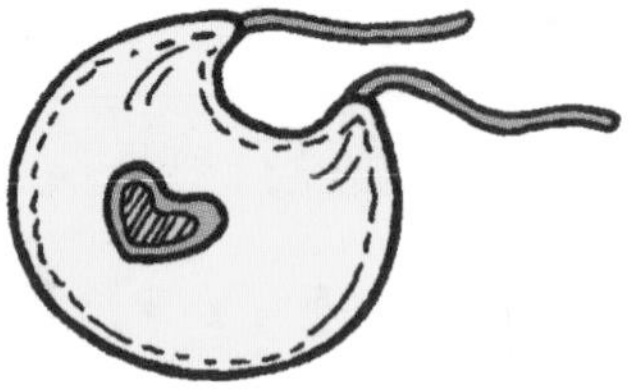

2. b __ b

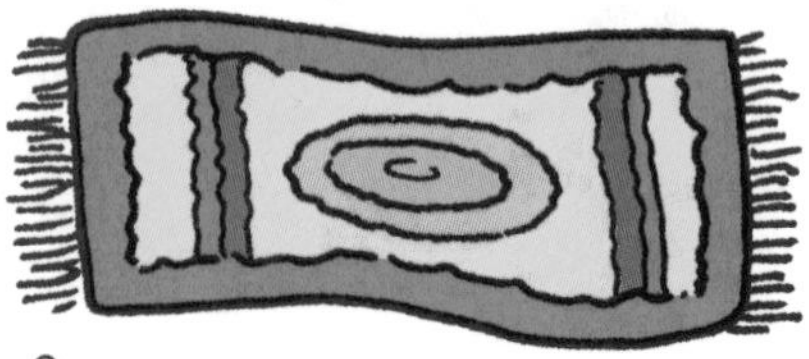

3. r __ g

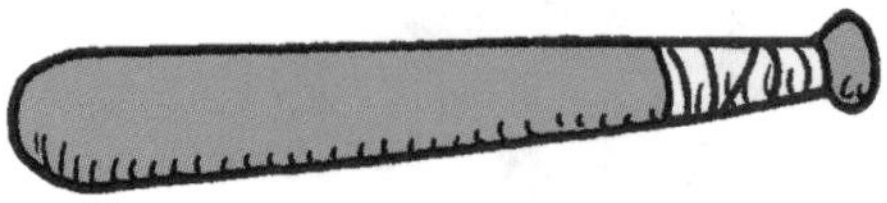

4. b __ t

5. b __ x

6. v __ n

7. b __ s

8. w __ b

Words with Long a

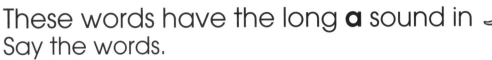

These words have the long **a** sound in .
Say the words.

rake	game	tape
vase	cake	gate

Write the answers on the lines.

1. You can put  in me.
   What am I?

   _____

2. You like to eat me.
   What am I?

   _____

3. I fix a torn page.
   What am I?

   _____

4. You use me to pile .
   What am I?

   _____

Write the words with the same **beginning** sound as .

_____   _____

_____   _____

Words with Long a

Write the long **a** word for each picture.
Say the words.

tape	rake	cake
game	vase	gate

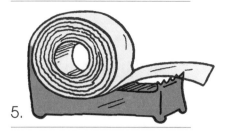

1. _____

2. _____

3. _____

4. _____

5. _____

6. _____

178

Words with Long e

These words have the long **e** sound in .
Say the words.

he	me	see
three	tree	she

Write two 2-letter words that rhyme with **bee**.

_____   _____

_____   _____

Write two 3-letter words that rhyme with **bee**.

_____   _____

_____   _____

Write the word for each picture.

1. _____   2. _____

_____   _____

Words with Long e

Write the long **e** words.
Then color the long **e** words in the picture green.

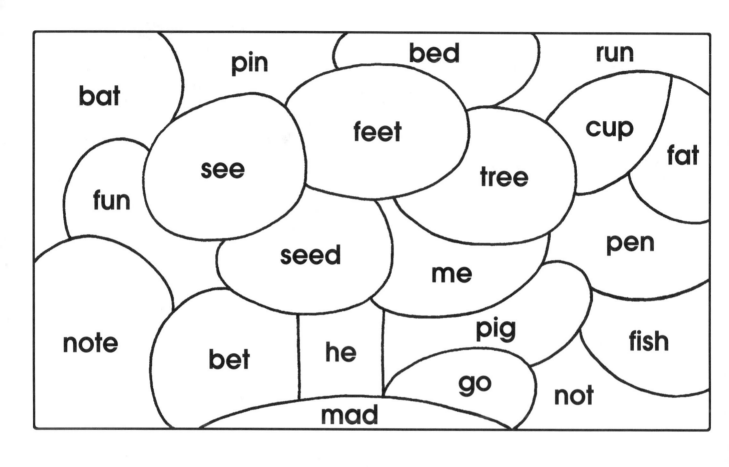

Words with Long **e**

Words with Long i

These words have the long **i** sound in .
Say the words.

kite	**tie**	**fine**
bike	**like**	**ride**

Write the answers on the lines.

1. You can fly me.
   What am I?

   _____

2. You can ride me.
   What am I?

   _____

3. I am something to wear.
   What am I?

   _____

Write the three other words that fit these shapes.

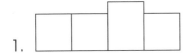 1. 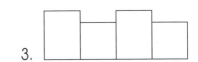 2.   3.

Words with Long i

Write the long **i** words.
Then color the long **i** words in the picture purple.

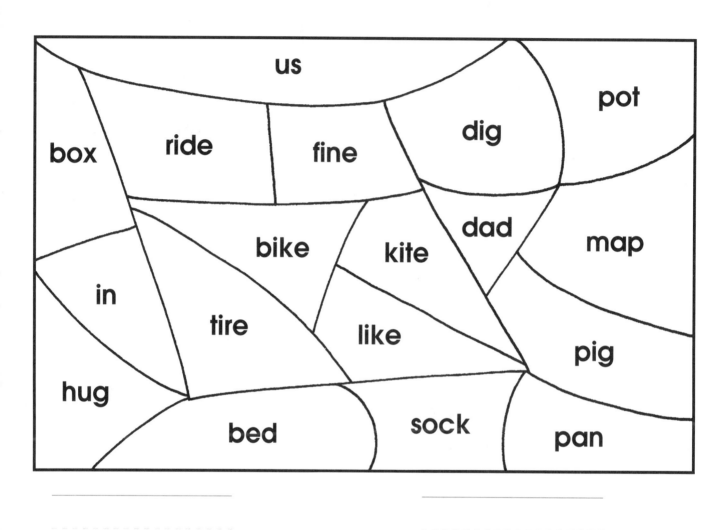

Words with Long o

These words have the long **o** sound in .
Say the words.

home	nose	joke
gold	fold	note

e	h	j	k	m	n	o	s	t
△	○	☆	◇	<	>	○	□	▯

Use the code to write the words.
Write the letter each shape shows.

> ○ ▯ △
_____

○ ○ < △
_____

1. _____   2. _____

☆ ○ ◇ △
_____

> ○ □ △
_____

3. _____   4. _____

Write the words that **rhyme** with **told**.

_____   _____

_____   _____

Words with Long o

Write the long **o** words.
Then color the long **o** words in the picture blue.

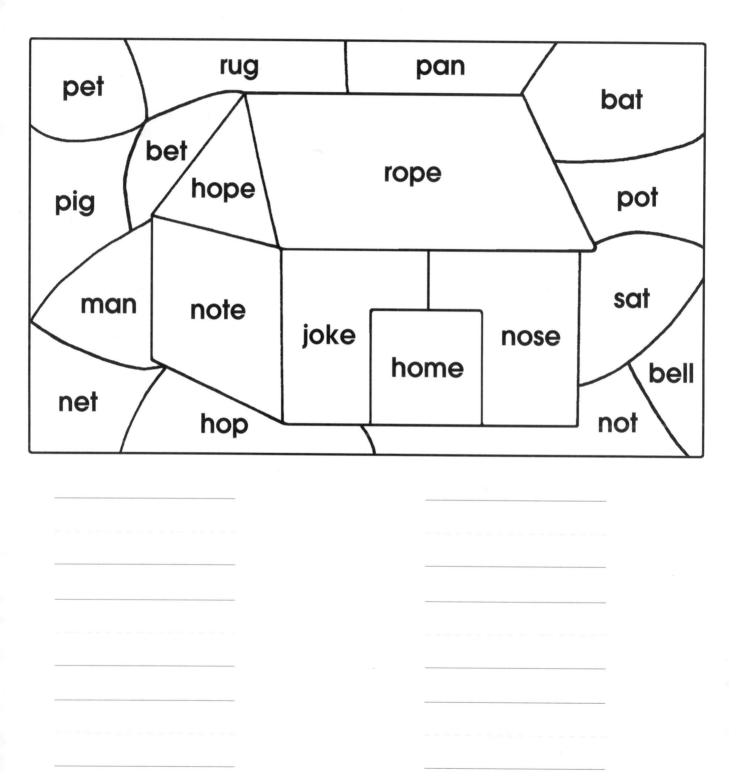

Words with Long u

These words have the long **u** sound in  .
Say the words.

cube	cute	huge
rule	mule	tube

c e g h l r t u b

△ ○ ☆ ◇ < > ○ □ ⬚

Use the code to write the words.
Write the letter each shape shows.

△ □ ○ ○

1. _____

○ □ ⬚ ○

2. _____

◇ □ ☆ ○

3. _____

> □ < ○

4. _____

Write the word for each picture.

1. _____

2. _____

Words with Long u

Write the long **u** words.
Then color the long **u** words in the picture red.

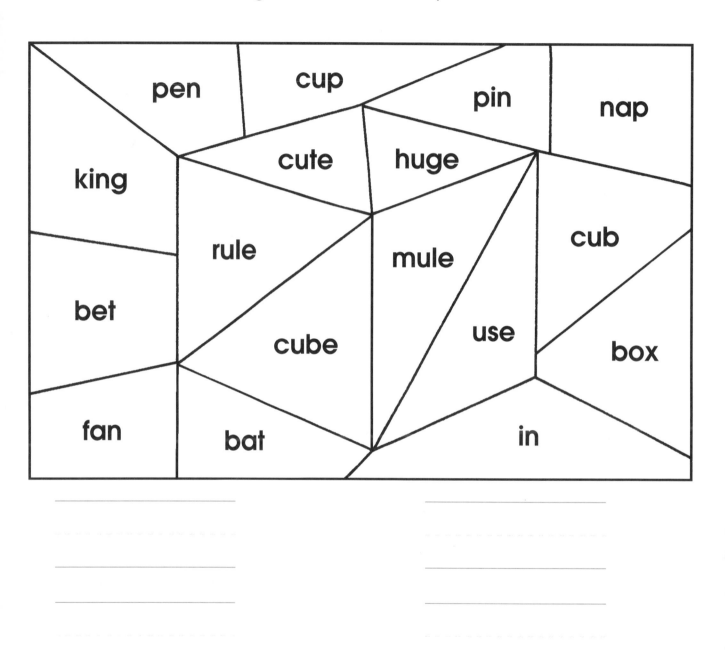

Review

Write the short **a** word in each blank.

nap   maps
bat   Dad

Sam walks to school.

_____

He learns about _____ .

At recess he plays with a ball and _____ .

_____

_____ drives him home.

_____

Sam is tired so he takes a _____ .

Circle all the short **e** words.

tent	bed	let	net
see	pen	she	key

Review

Write the answers on the lines.

| fox | sock | box | pot |

1. You put me on your foot.
   What am I?

_____

2. I hold toys for you.
   What am I?

_____

3. Mom uses me to cook.
   What am I?

_____

4. I am an animal.
   What am I?

_____

a b c d e f g h i j k l m n o p q r s t u v w x y z
Write the words in alphabetical order.

| us | hug | sun |

1. _____   2. _____   3. _____

Review

Write the **a** word in each blank.

game	**rake**
vase	**gate**

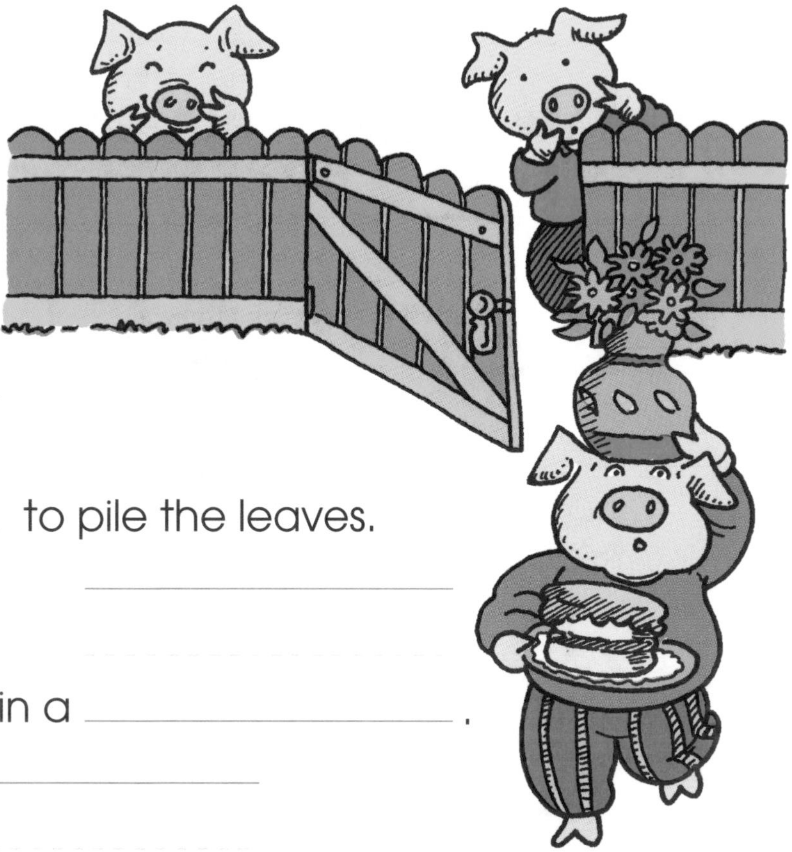

Bring a ________________ to pile the leaves.

We will pick flowers to put in a ________________ .

Then we can play a ________________ of tag.

Don't go past the ________________ .

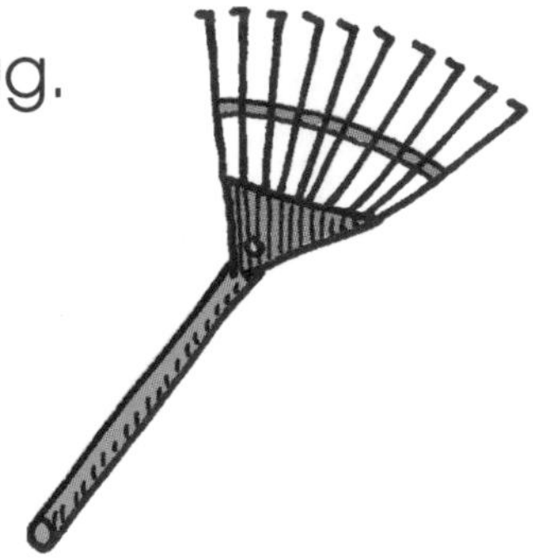

Circle all the long **e** words.

net	**tree**	**he**	**seed**
see	**get**	**ten**	**bee**

Review

Write the answers on the lines.

nose	rope	note	home

1. You can tie things with me. What am I?

_____

2. You use me to smell. What am I?

_____

3. You live in me. What am I?

_____

4. You write me. What am I?

_____

a b c d e f g h i j k l m n o p q r s t u v w x y z
Write the words in alphabetical order.

mule	rule	cute

1. _____   2. _____   3. _____

Review

Write five sentences using one of these words in each sentence.

game	home	in
like	Dad	

1. _____

_____

2. _____

_____

3. _____

_____

4. _____

_____

5. _____

_____

Answer Key

Page 161
1. fan   2. pie
3. rain   4. cat
5. hat   6. man
7. tie   8. kite

Page 162
1. leaf   2. dog
3. ball   4. queen
5. yarn   6. goat
7. nine   8. soap

Page 163
1. pig   2. sun
3. cup   4. tub
5. nail   6. fox
7. bear   8. drum

Page 164
1. bed   2. seal
3. car   4. elf
5. zero   6. bus
7. cat   8. book

Page 165
1. man   2. mop
3. pen   4. sun
5. bib   6. pan
7. bug   8. ten

Page 166
1. pan   2. map
   fan   nap

1. dad   2. bat

Page 167
fan, map,
pan, bat,
dad, nap

Page 168
1. net   2. ten
3. pen   4. pet

1. bed   2. bell

Page 169
pet, pen, ten,
bed, bell, net

Page 170
1. in
2. his

big, pig,
dig, wig

Page 171
in, his, wig,
big, pig, dig

Page 172
sock, top, box

pot, not, lot

Page 173
box, hot, sock,
fox, pot, lot

Page 174
1. up
2. sun
3. run

1. hug   2. rug   3. us

Page 175
1. rug   2. up
3. sun   4. hug
5. bus   6. run

Page 176
1. bell   2. bib
3. rug   4. bat
5. box   6. van
7. bus   8. web

Page 177
1. vase
2. cake
3. tape
4. rake

game, gate

Page 178
1. vase   2. gate
3. rake   4. cake
5. tape   6. game

Page 179
he, me

see, she

1. tree   2. three

Page 180
see, feet,
me, tree,
he, seed

Page 181
1. kite
2. bike
3. tie

1. ride   2. fine   3. like

Page 182
kite, ride,
fine, tire,
bike, like

Page 183
1. note   2. home
3. joke   4. nose

fold, gold

Page 184
nose, rope,
home, note,
hope, joke

Page 185
1. cute   2. tube
3. huge   4. rule

1. mule   2. cube

Page 186
cube, use,
rule, huge,
cute, mule

Page 187
Sam walks to school.
He learns about **maps**.
At recess he plays with a ball and **bat**.
Dad drives him home.
Sam is tired so he takes a **nap**.

tent, bed, pen, let, net

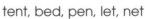

Page 188
1. sock
2. box
3. pot
4. fox

1. hug   2. sun   3. us

Page 189
Bring a **rake** to pile the leaves.
We will pick flowers to put in a **vase**.
Then we can play a **game** of tag.
Don't go past the **gate**.

see, tree, he, seed, bee

Page 190
1. rope
2. nose
3. home
4. note

1. cute   2. mule   3. rule

Page 191
Automatic fill-in.

Short a Words

Put a letter in place of each number to finish the sentence.

cat	Dad	hat
sat	bad	mad

1 2 3 4 5 6 7 8 9
D d b a m c t s h

___ ___ ___ got ___ ___ ___ when the
1   4   2   5   4   2

___ ___ ___ ___ ___ ___ ___ ___ ___
3   4   2   6   4   7   8   4   7

on his ___ ___ ___ .
9   4   7

Write three words that end with **t**.

_____   _____   _____

Write three words that end with **d**.

_____   _____   _____

Short e Words

Read the clues. Write the word.

1. it + en – i =

2. bib + ed – bi =

3. up + en – u =

4. him + en – hi =

5. now + et – no =

6. pig + et – pi =

7. hay + es – ha =

8. far + ed – fa =

Write two words that end with **t**.

_____   _____

Write two words that end with **d**.

_____   _____

Write two words that end with **n**.

_____   _____

Short i Words

Write the word that fits each shape.

six	sit	fish
big	pig	did
give	his	

1. ▢▢▢

2. ▢▢▢

3. ▢▢▢

4. ▢▢▢▢

5. ▢▢▢▢

6. ▢▢▢

7. ▢▢▢

8. ▢▢▢

Write the word from the box that **rhymes** with each word below.

1. **big** _____

2. **fix** _____

3. **live** _____

4. **hit** _____

5. **dish** _____

6. **hid** _____

Short o Words

Write the word to finish each sentence.
Then circle each word in the puzzle.

fox	box	pop
top	mom	hot
job	hop	

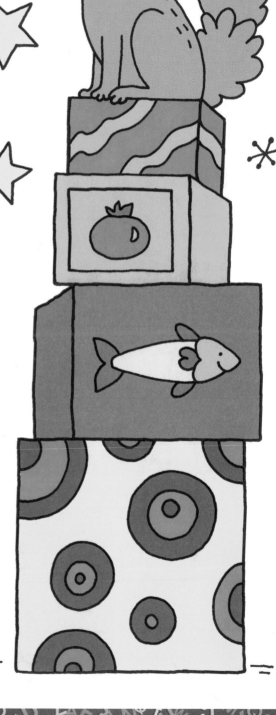

1. The dog looks like a _____ .

2. The soup is too _____ to eat.

3. How far can you _____?

4. We had hot dogs and _____ .

5. His _____ said he can go.

6. It is my _____ to set the table.

7. What is in the _____?

8. The book is on the _____ shelf.

```
H O T J O B
O M O M X O
P O P F O X
```

Short u Words

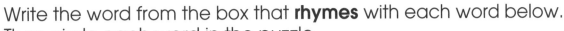

Write the word from the box that **rhymes** with each word below.
Then circle each word in the puzzle.

nut	up	gum
bug	bus	tub
duck	fun	

1. run

2. hug

3. rub

4. but

_____

5. luck

6. cup

7. us

8. hum

_____

```
R D U C K
F U N U P
N B U G R
R U T U B
C S A M L
```

Compound Words

Two words that are put together to make one word become a **compound word**.

Circle the two words in each **compound word**.

something   snowball

everywhere   anyone

inside   cannot

maybe   sunshine

herself   birthday

Match a word from the **A** list to a word from the **B** list to make a **compound word**.

A	+	B
1. moon		plane
2. rain		light
3. air		ground
4. foot		fly
5. butter		coat
6. play		ball

moonlight

Words with a, aw, o

Put a letter in place of each number to make words.

call	frog	saw
small	dog	draw
jog	walk	

1 2 3 4 5 6 7 8 9 10 11 12 13
s c a f d j w g o l r m k

What do you $\frac{}{2}$ $\frac{}{3}$ $\frac{}{10}$ $\frac{}{10}$ a $\frac{}{1}$ $\frac{}{12}$ $\frac{}{3}$ $\frac{}{10}$ $\frac{}{10}$

$\frac{}{5}$ $\frac{}{9}$ $\frac{}{8}$ that takes a $\frac{}{4}$ $\frac{}{11}$ $\frac{}{9}$ $\frac{}{8}$ for a

$\frac{}{7}$ $\frac{}{3}$ $\frac{}{10}$ $\frac{}{13}$?

A $\frac{}{4}$ $\frac{}{11}$ $\frac{}{9}$ $\frac{}{8}$ - $\frac{}{6}$ $\frac{}{9}$ $\frac{}{8}$ ger.

Words with ar, or

Put a letter in place of each number to make words.

far	hard	short
car	more	store
start	wore	

1 2 3 4 5 6 7 8 9 10 11 12
m w s e c a r t h o f d

1. 1 + 10 + 7 + 4

_____

2. 5 + 6 + 7

_____

3. 3 + 9 + 10 + 7 + 8

_____

4. 9 + 6 + 7 + 12

_____

5. 11 + 6 + 7

_____

6. 3 + 8 + 10 + 7 + 4

_____

7. 3 + 8 + 6 + 7 + 8

_____

8. 2 + 10 + 7 + 4

_____

Words with er, or, ir, ur

Read the clues to finish the puzzle.

letter	bird	turn	mother
word	hurt	work	

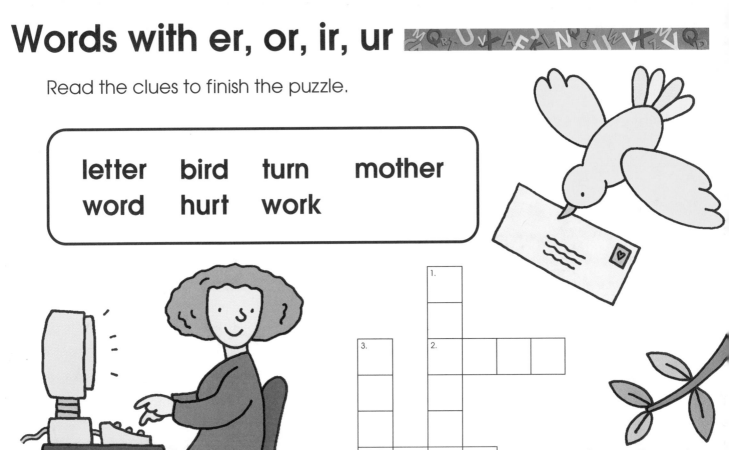

Across

2. move around a center

4. do harm to

5. something that is said

6. an animal with wings and feathers

Down

1. a note written to a person

3. a female parent

5. job

Sight Words

Help each bee to find its flower.

Write each word on the correct flower.

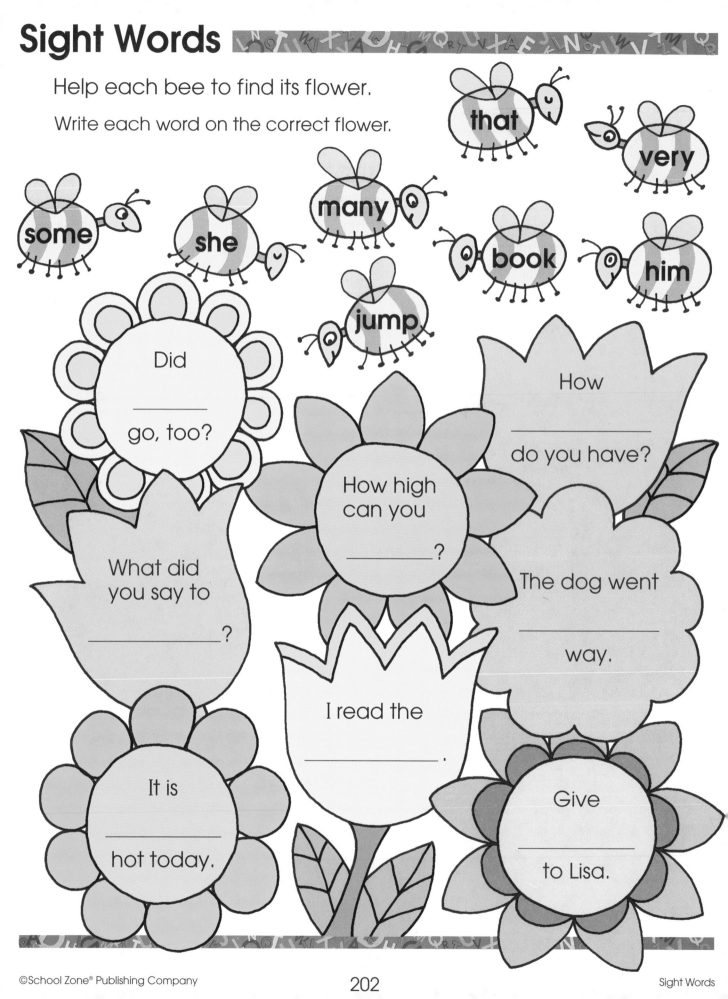

that

very

some

she

many

book

him

jump

Did
_____
go, too?

How high
can you
_____?

How
_____
do you have?

What did
you say to
_____?

I read the
_____.

The dog went
_____
way.

It is
_____
hot today.

Give
_____
to Lisa.

Sight Words

Write the word for each clue.
Then read the letters in the box to answer the riddle.

go   down
big   right
bottom

1. opposite of up _ _ _ _

2. opposite of little _ _ _

3. opposite of stop _ _

4. opposite of left _ _ _ _ _

5. opposite of top _ _ _ _ _ _

The opposite of day is _____.

Words with c, k, ck

Write the word to finish each sentence.
Then read the clues to finish the puzzle.

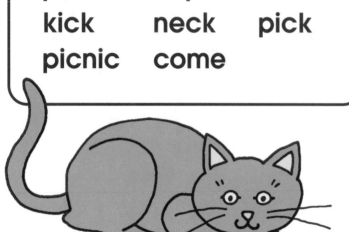

pack	cup	kitten
kick	neck	pick
picnic	come	

Across

1. Our dog did not _____ with us.

2. Did you _____ your toothbrush?

3. We had a _____ at the lake.

5. How far can you _____ the ball?

6. The _____ drinks milk.

Down

1. The _____ broke.

2. Did you _____ berries?

4. A giraffe has a long _____ .

Double Consonants

Write the word that fits each shape.

pass	rabbit	off
funny	puppy	eggs
tell	happy	

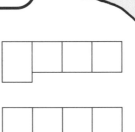

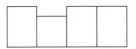

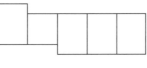

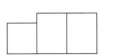

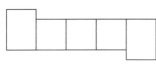

Read the clues. Write words from the box.

1. an animal that hops _____
2. opposite of on _____
3. silly _____
4. glad; pleased _____
5. say _____
6. go by _____
7. what a hen lays _____
8. a young dog _____

Blends cl, dr, sm, st, sw

Finish the puzzle with a **rhyming** word.

smile   sting   dress

class   smell   drag

Across

2. thing

4. mile

5. mess

Down

1. flag

2. tell

3. grass

Fill in the **blend** to finish the word.

___ ___ own

___ ___ an

___ ___ ar

Words Ending with mp, nd, nt, sk, st

Put a letter in place of each number to make words.

send	**hand**	**just**
stamp	**went**	**test**
desk	**ask**	

1 2 3 4 5 6 7 8 9 10 11 12 13
s m t a d e p j h n k w u

1. 9 + 4 + 10 + 5

_____

2. 4 + 1 + 11

_____

3. 1 + 6 + 10 + 5

_____

4. 5 + 6 + 1 + 11

_____

5. 1 + 3 + 4 + 2 + 7

_____

6. 3 + 6 + 1 + 3

_____

7. 12 + 6 + 10 + 3

_____

8. 8 + 13 + 1 + 3

_____

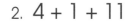

Words Beginning with ch, sh, th, wh

Read the clues to finish the puzzle.

think   when   chop   shut
thin   where check shop

Across

1. close

2. cut into pieces

3. use the mind

4. at what time

Down

1. a store

2. to test if true

3. slim

4. at what place

Words Ending with ch, ng, sh, th

Write the word for each clue.
Then read the letters in the box to answer the riddle.

inch	branch
bring	long
fish	path

1. a water animal   __ __ __ __

2. a walkway   __ __ __ __

3. part of a tree   __ __ __ __ __ __

4. carry   __ __ __ __ __

5. part of a foot   __ __ __ __

6. opposite of short   __ __ __ __

I come after winter.
What am I? _____

Add the missing letters to make words.

1. bran __ __   2. lo __ __   3. pa __ __

4. bri __ __   5. in __ __   6. fi __ __

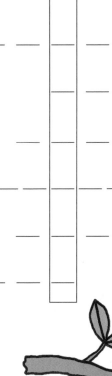

Vowel-Consonant-e

Many words with a long vowel sound are spelled with vowel-consonant-**e** (mad - made).

Add an **-e** to each word to make a new word.

1. at __

2. kit __

3. pin __

4. hug __

5. dim __

6. mad __

Help fly the kites.

Write each word from above on the correct kite.

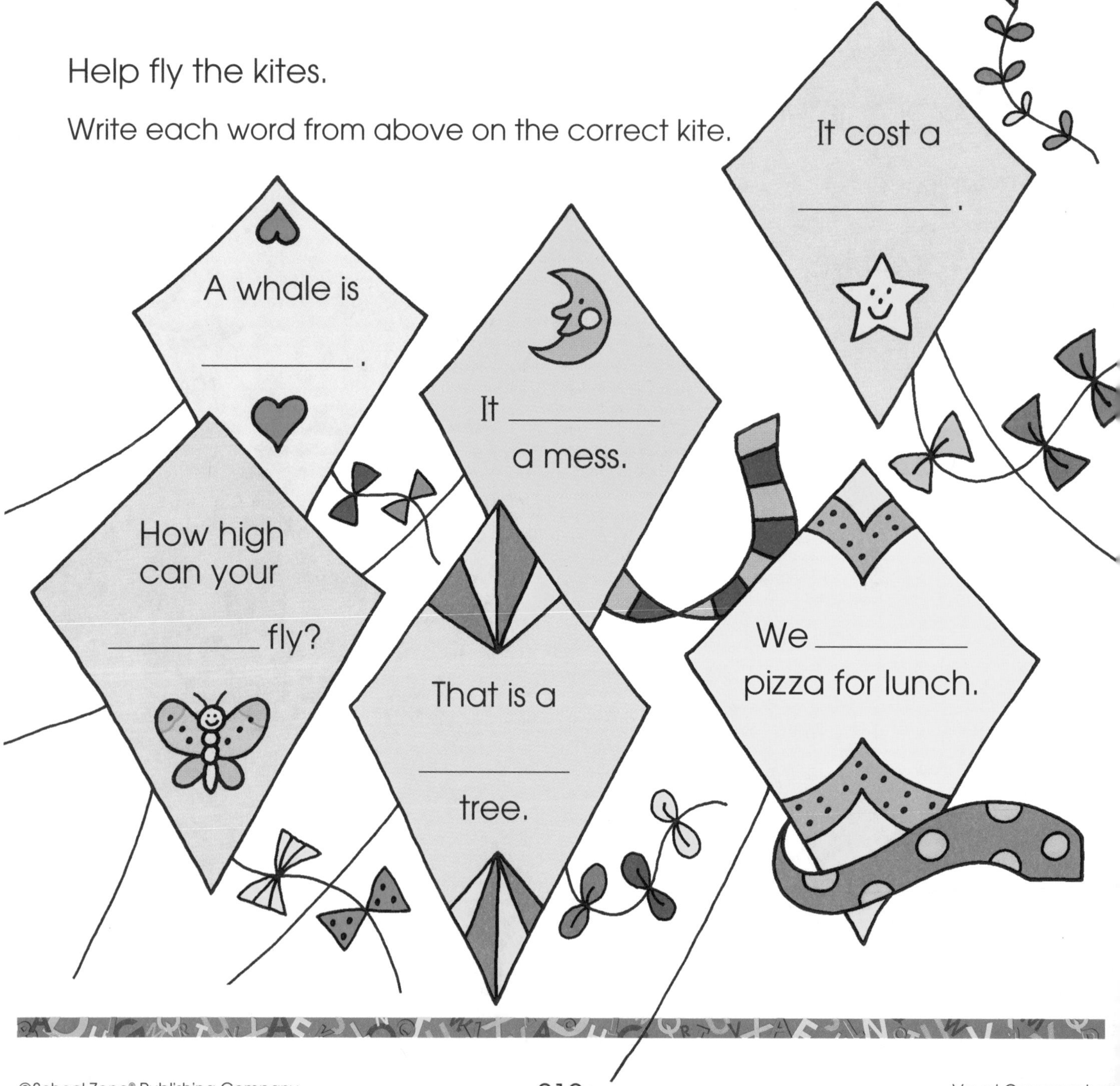

It cost a

_____ .

A whale is

_____ .

It _____

a mess.

How high can your

_____ fly?

That is a

_____

tree.

We _____

pizza for lunch.

Vowel-Consonant-**e**

Vowel-Consonant-e

Write the word for each clue.
Then read the letters in the box to answer the riddle.

home	dime	pine	those
nine	cute	save	make

1. keep ___ _ _ _

2. pretty _ ___ _ _

3. one more than eight _ _ ___ _

4. plural of that _ _ _ ___ _

5. where a person lives ___ _ _ _

6. a 10¢ coin _ ___ _ _

7. a kind of tree _ _ ___ _

8. build _ _ _ ___

I brighten your day.
What am I?

_____

Add the missing letters to make a word.

1. c __ t __   2. s __ v __   3. h __ m __   4. m __ k __

5. d __ m __   6. th __ s __   7. n __ n __   8. p __ n __

Words with Long a, ai, ay

Fill the **a** train with long **a** words.
Write the missing letters to make a long **a** word.

wait	mail	paint
day	play	rain
stay	say	

st _ _

pl _ _ _

s _ _ _

p _ _ nt

d _ _ _

r _ _ n

m _ _ l

w _ _ t

Add the missing letters to finish the sentence.

1. Did your mom s _ _ you could pl _ _?

2. Can you st _ _ all d _ _?

3. Do not w _ _ t in the r _ _ n.

Words with Long e, ea, ee

Read the clues. Write the word.

1. if + eel – i = _____

2. far + ead – fa = _____

3. he + at – h = _____

4. is + he – i = _____

5. it + eeth – i = _____

6. it + eam – i = _____

7. tea + ch – t = _____

8. kick + eep – kic = _____

Write two long **e** words with **ee**.

_____ _____

Write two long **e** words with **ea**.

_____ _____

Words with Long i, y, igh

Write the word that fits each shape.

try	mind	right
light	cry	kind
high	why	

1.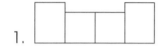

2.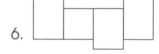

3.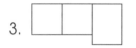

4.

5.

6.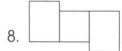

7.

8.

Read the clue. Write the word.

1. far above

2. not heavy

3. call loudly

_____

_____

_____

4. correct

5. friendly

6. for what reason

_____

_____

_____

7. put to a test

8. brain

_____

_____

Words with Long o, oa, ow

Write the word for each clue.
Then read the letters in the box to answer the riddle.

own	told	show	both
coat	grow	goat	

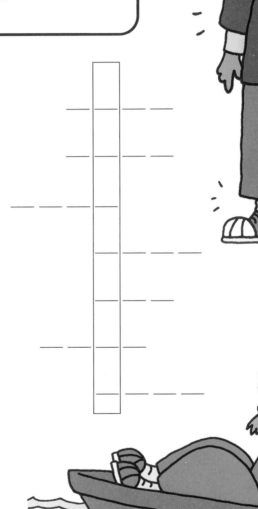

1. get bigger _ _ _ _

2. worn over clothes _ _ _ _

3. put in sight _ _ _ _

4. one, then another _ _ _ _

5. have _ _ _ _

6. a farm animal _ _ _ _

7. said; put into words _ _ _ _

I float on water.
What am I?

_____

Add the missing letters to make a word.

1. gr __ __   2. sh __ __   3. __ wn   4. t __ ld

5. c __ __ t   6. b __ th   7. g __ __ t

Words with oo, ew

Read the clues. Write the word.

1. if + ood – i =

2. is + oon – i =

3. for + oom – fo =

4. it + ool – i =

5. in + ew – i =

6. now + ho – no =

7. mom + oon – mo =

8. ofl + ew – o =

Add the missing letters to make a word.

1. n __ __

2. f __ __ d

3. wh __

4. t __ __ l

5. fl __ __

6. m __ __ n

7. s __ __ n

8. r __ __ m

Words Ending with er

Read the clues to finish the sentence.
Then circle each word in the puzzle.

after	over	flower
under	water	better
sister	answer	

```
A F T E R O A
S L B K J V N
I O I S T E S
S W A T E R W
T E H C T T E
E R U N D E R
R B E T T E R
```

1. The ball went _____ the chair.

2. It is your turn _____ Sara.

3. May I have a drink of _____?

4. A rose is a _____ .

5. Can you _____ the question?

6. Her _____ is six today.

7. Sara feels _____ today.

8. The cat jumped _____ the fence.

Words Ending with y

Y has an **e** sound at the end of some words.

Read the clues to finish the puzzle.

penny   kitty   pretty   easy
silly   lucky   funny   baby

Across

3. causing laughter

5. not hard

7. foolish

8. very young child

Down

1. cute

2. having good luck

4. one cent

6. baby cat

218

Adding -ing

If a word ends in **e**, drop the **e** and add **-ing**.

Write the word to finish each sentence.

hide	hope
come	make
smile	write

1. Is Peter _____ with us?

2. I keep _____ it will not rain.

3. The cat is _____ from the dog.

4. Dad is _____ a birdhouse.

5. Tina is _____ a story.

6. Everyone was _____ during the play.

Write each word with an **-ing** ending.

			i	n	g
			i	n	g
			i	n	g
			i	n	g
			i	n	g
			i	n	g

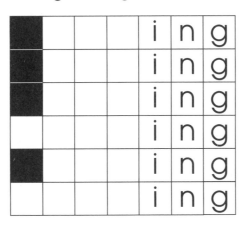

Adding -s, -es

Add **-s** or **-es** to make a word name more than one.
Add **-s** to most words. Add **-es** to words that end in **ch**, **sh** and **x**.

Finish the puzzle with a rhyming word.

books   boxes
dogs   dishes
bells   inches

Across

2. tells

3. wishes

5. hogs

Down

1. foxes

2. looks

4. pinches

Adding -es

The ending **-es** can be added to some words to name more than one.

If a word ends with a consonant and **y**, change the **y** to **i** and add **-es**.

1. one baby

two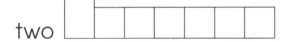

2. one penny

two

3. one berry

two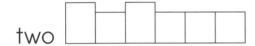

4. one candy

two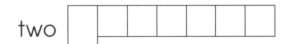

5. one puppy

two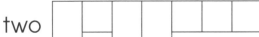

6. one butterfly

two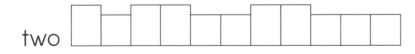

Adding -ing or -ed

Some words end with one vowel and one consonant. To get the short vowel sound, double the final consonant before adding **-ing** or **-ed** (hop - hopped - hopping).

Write the correct ending for each word to finish the sentence.

sled	rub	grab
skip	bat	hug
nap	hop	

1. The rabbit (hop) into its hutch. _____

2. Jo (bat) in the winning run. _____

3. A good exercise is (skip) rope. _____

4. The baby is (nap) in her crib. _____

5. I (grab) the dish before it fell. _____

6. My bicycle tire is (rub) against the fender. _____

7. The players (hug) each other after the game. _____

8. The snow is perfect for (sled). _____

Answer Key

Page 193

Dad got **mad** when the **bad cat sat** on his **hat**.

Page 194

1. ten
2. bed
3. pen
4. men
5. wet
6. get
7. yes
8. red

Page 195

1. did
2. pig
3. big
4. fish
5. give
6. sit
7. six
8. his

1. pig
2. six
3. give
4. sit
5. fish
6. did

Page 196

1. fox
2. hot
3. hop
4. pop
5. mom
6. job
7. box
8. top

H O T J O B
O M O M X O
P O P F O X

Page 197

1. fun
2. bug
3. tub
4. nut
5. duck
6. up
7. bus
8. gum

R D U C K
F U N U P
N B U G R
R U T U B
C S A M L

Page 198

some thing   snow ball
every where   any one
in side   can not
may be   sun shine
her self   birth day

1. moonlight
2. raincoat
3. airplane
4. football
5. butterfly
6. playground

Page 199

What do you **call** a **small dog** that takes a **frog** for a **walk**? A **frog-jog**ger.

Page 200

1. more
2. car
3. short
4. hard
5. far
6. store
7. start
8. wore

Page 201

Across
2. turn
4. hurt
5. word
6. bird

Down
1. letter
3. mother
5. work

Page 202

Did **she** go, to?
How high can you **jump**?
How **many** do you have?
What did you say to **him**?
The dog went **that** way.
It is **very** hot today.
I read the **book**.
Give **some** to Lisa.

Page 203

1. down
2. big
3. go
4. right
5. bottom

night

Page 204

Across
1. come
2. pack
3. picnic
5. kick
6. kitten

Down
1. cup
2. pick
4. neck

Page 205

tell   pass
off   egg
funny   happy
puppy   rabbit

1. rabbit
2. off
3. funny
4. happy
5. tell
6. pass
7. eggs
8. puppy

Page 206

Across
2. sting
4. smile
5. dress

Down
1. drag
2. smell
3. class

clown **sw**an **st**ar

Page 207

1. hand
2. ask
3. send
4. desk
5. stamp
6. test
7. went
8. just

Page 208

Across
1. shut
2. chop
3. think
4. when

Down
1. shop
2. check
3. thin
4. where

Answer Key

Page 209
1. fish
2. path
3. branch
4. bring
5. inch
6. long

spring

1. bran**ch** 2. lo**ng** 3. pa**th**
4. bri**ng** 5. in**ch** 6. fi**sh**

Page 210
1. ate 2. kite 3. pine
4. huge 5. dime 6. made

A **whale** is huge.
It **made** a mess.
It cost a **dime**.
How high can your **kite** fly?
That is a **pine** tree.
We **ate** pizza for lunch.

Page 211
1. save
2. cute
3. nine
4. those
5. home
6. dime
7. pine
8. make

sunshine

1. c**u**te 2. s**a**ve 3. h**o**me 4. m**a**ke
5. d**i**me 6. th**o**se 7. n**i**ne 8. p**i**ne

Page 212
st**ay**, pl**ay**, s**ay**, p**ai**nt,
d**ay**, r**ai**n, m**ai**l, w**ai**t

1. Did your mom s**ay** you could pl**ay**?
2. Can you st**ay** all d**ay**?
3. Do not w**ai**t in the r**ai**n.

Page 213
1. feel
2. read
3. eat
4. she
5. teeth
6. team
7. each
8. keep

Page 214
1. kind 2. why
3. cry 4. light
5. right 6. high
7. mind 8. try

1. high 2. light 3. cry
4. right 5. kind 6. why
7. try 8. mind

Page 215
1. grow
2. coat
3. show
4. both
5. own
6. goat
7. told

rowboat

1. gr**ow** 2. sh**ow** 3. **ow**n 4. t**o**ld
5. c**oa**t 6. b**o**th 7. g**oa**t

Page 216
1. food
2. soon
3. room
4. tool
5. new
6. who
7. moon
8. flew

1. n**ew** 2. f**oo**d 3. wh**o** 4. t**oo**l
5. fl**ew** 6. m**oo**n 7. s**oo**n 8. r**oo**m

Page 217
1. under
2. after
3. water
4. flower
5. answer
6. sister
7. better
8. over

Page 218
Across
3. funny
5. easy
7. silly
8. baby

Down
1. pretty
2. lucky
4. penny
6. kitty

Page 219
1. coming
2. hoping
3. hiding
4. making
5. writing
6. smiling

Page 220
Across
2. bells
3. dishes
5. dogs

Down
1. boxes
2. books
4. inches

Page 221
1. babies
2. pennies
3. berries
4. candies
5. puppies
6. butterflies

Page 222
1. hopped
2. batted
3. skipping
4. napping
5. grabbed
6. rubbing
7. hugged
8. sledding

I Can Read!

◆ Write a word or number to finish each sentence.

1. My name is _____ .

2. I am _____ years old.

3. I have _____ brothers.

4. I have _____ sisters.

5. I can _____ this book!

◆ Draw a picture of your family.

At the Park

◆ Look at the picture. Write how many of each you see.

1. swings

_____
- - - - -
_____

2. seesaws

_____
- - - - -
_____

3. slides

_____
- - - - -
_____

4. benches

_____
- - - - -
_____

◆ Underline the one that has more.

5.

   swings   or   benches

6.

   benches   or   slides

7.

   slides   or   seesaws

8.

   seesaws   or   swings

A Party!

Come to a party!
Please come.

What: Jenny's birthday party
Where: Jenny's house
Date: May 5
Time: 2:00 PM

◆ Underline the correct answers.

1. Who is having the party?   Jenny   birthday
2. What is the party for?   birthday   house
3. Where will the party be?   Jenny   house
4. What day is the party?   May 5   2:00 PM
5. What time is the party?   May 5   2:00 PM
6. What will you take to the party?

_____

_____

I will take _____

_____

_____

_____

Drawing Conclusions/Decoding

Get a Pet!

◆ **Read the picture story.**

Do you want a dog? Go to

a pet store. Pick out a dog.

Take your dog home.

What will you name your dog?

◆ **Show how to buy a pet. Number the pictures 1, 2, 3, and 4 to show the order.**

Pick out a pet.

Take your pet home.

Go to a pet store.

Name your pet.

Shoes!

◆ **Draw a line from each sentence to the correct shoes.**

1. These are red.

A.

2. These have laces.

B.

3. Those are purple.

C.

4. Those are for races.

D.

5. These are for babies.

E.

6. These are for snow.

F.

7. These are for clowns.

G.

8. Those warm your toes!

H.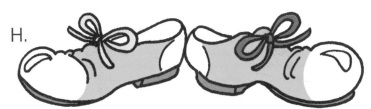

Which One Does Not Belong?

◆ Mark an **X** on the one in each group
that does not belong.

1.

2.

3.

4.

5.

6.

Classifying/Picture Clues

Opposites Puzzle

◆ **Read the clues.**
Write the opposites in the puzzle.
Use the words in the box.

Across ▶

1. found
3. hot
5. in

Down ▼

1. right
2. stop
4. up

cold
down
go
left
lost
out

Decoding/Opposites

Find The Message!

◆ **Follow the directions.**
   Then read the words that are left.

1. Color the **Y** boxes **red**.
2. Color the **C** boxes **blue**.
3. Color the **J** boxes orange.
4. Color the **H** boxes **brown**.
5. Color the **Z** boxes **black**.

Y	I	C	J	Z	L	I	K	E	C
R	E	D	C	J	Z	Y	H	J	Y
H	Z	Y	F	L	O	W	E	R	S
A	N	D	Y	P	U	R	P	L	E
C	J	B	A	L	L	O	O	N	S

◆ **Write the words. Show the message to someone.**

_____

_____

_____

Write a Story!

◆ Draw one more thing that belongs in each group.

The Beach

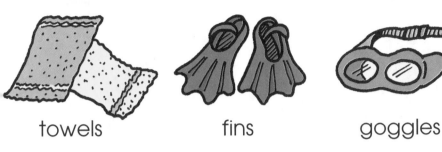

towels   fins   goggles

A Picnic

drinks   dishes   food

◆ Use two words from above to write a riddle.
Read your riddle to a friend.

I am going somewhere. I will take some

_____

_____

_____ and

_____

_____

some _____ . Where am I going?

_____

_____

I am going _____ .

In My Garden

Please Take Care with My Flowers

◆ **Color the squares to show how many.**

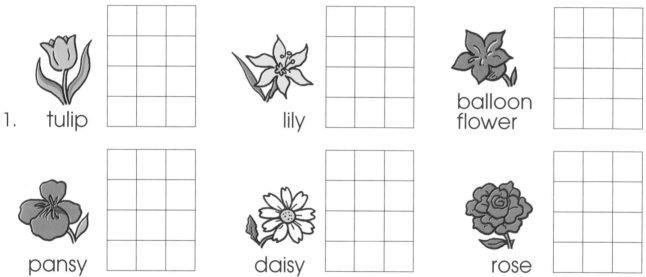

1. tulip

lily

balloon flower

pansy

daisy

rose

◆ **Which flower do you see? Check the boxes.**

2. the most

☐ tulip   ☐ rose

3. the least

☐ daisy   ☐ balloon flower

4. the same number as the tulip

☐ pansy   ☐ lily

◆ **Which flower do you like best?**

_____

5. I like the _____ best.

Picture Clues/Comparisons

Make a Sandwich!

◆ **Read how to make a sandwich.**

Ham and Cheese Sandwich

What you need: two pieces of bread, some ham, some cheese

1. Get two pieces of bread.
2. Put some ham on one piece.
3. Put some cheese on the ham.
4. Put one slice of bread on top.
5. Eat!

◆ **Number the pictures 1, 2, 3, and 4 to show the order.**

Mystery Bus

◆ **Read the picture story.**

Amy got on the bus.

It was her first bus ride ever.

The driver showed Amy her seat.

The bus stopped many times.

Other kids got on.

Where was the bus going?

◆ **Underline the correct answers.**

1. What did Amy get on?   bus   boat
2. Who showed Amy where to sit?   mother   driver
3. Who got on when the bus stopped?   dogs   kids
4. Did Amy ride a bus before?   yes   no
5. Did the bus stop a lot?   yes   no
6. Where was the bus going?

_____

_ _

The bus was going to _____

Making Predictions/Picture Clues

Hats!

◆ **Draw a line from each sentence to the correct hat.**

1. Wear a tall one to cook.   A.

2. Wear this to the game.   B.

3. Wear a helmet to ride.   C.

4. Wear a hat with a name.   D.

5. Wear a hat that is soft.   E.

6. Wear one that is gray.   F.

7. Wear a hat made of straw.   G.

8. Wear a Happy Birthday hat!   H.

Which Is Real?

◆ Underline the animals that look real.

1.

2.

3.

4.

What Do You Know?

◆ **Read the clues.**
Write the words in the puzzle.
Use the words in the box.

cold
dry
new
open
closed
hot
old

Across ▶

1. No one is in the school.
   The school is __.

5. I got these shoes long ago.
   These shoes are __.

6. Mom just bought a car.
   The car is __.

Down ▼

1. It is snowing outside.
   It is __.

2. People are shopping.
   The store is __.

3. I wiped water off the floor.
   The floor is __.

4. Dinner is cooking in the oven.
   The oven is __.

Who is it?

◆ **Read the clues. Write each name under the correct picture.**

Sara has a green hat.

Mia always wears red.

Kenji never wears blue.

Mimi likes to paint.

Ty has purple shoes.

Bob wears the color of the sky.

1. _____

_ _ _ _ _ _ _ _ _ _ _ _

_____

2. _____

_ _ _ _ _ _ _ _ _ _ _ _

_____

3. _____

_ _ _ _ _ _ _ _ _ _ _ _

_____

4. _____

_ _ _ _ _ _ _ _ _ _ _ _

_____

5. _____

_ _ _ _ _ _ _ _ _ _ _ _

_____

6. _____

_ _ _ _ _ _ _ _ _ _ _ _

_____

Play Toss The Penny!

Play Toss the Penny.
You need ten pennies and a
muffin tin.

Put the tin near a wall.
Stand about ten steps away.
Toss a penny. Try to get it in a hole.
How many pennies can you get in?

◆ **Underline the correct answers.**

1. Where should you put the muffin tin?

near a wall

under a bed

2. Where should you stand?

5 steps away

10 steps away

3. What should you do with the penny?

toss it

spin it

4. Where do you want the penny to go?

in your pocket

in a hole

◆ **Circle how many pennies you need to play this game.**

5.

Following Directions/Decoding Skills

Silly Man!

I know a silly man
who walks on his hands.
He has a silly car,
but it doesn't go too far.
And in his silly town,
shops are upside down.
Tell me if you can,
when you see this silly man.

◆ **Underline the correct answers.**

1. Which one is the silly man?

2. Which car is his?

3. Which hat is his?

4. Which pet is his?

242

Context Clues/Following Directions

What's Next?

◆ **Look at each picture.**
Then draw what happens next.

1. It is time to cool off.

2. It is time to play.

3. It is time for lunch.

4. The sun gets hot.

Find a Rhyme!

Words that rhyme sound the same at the end.
Pan and **can** rhyme. **Mike** and **bike** rhyme.

◆ Cross out the word that does not rhyme in each row.

1. dog   log   bird   hog

2. man   pin   fan   can

3. boy   boat   coat   goat

4. two   shoe   blue   bow

Get Through the Maze!

◆ **Put the crayons away. Follow the directions.**

Make a **red** line to put the **red** crayon away.

Make a **yellow** line to put the **yellow** crayon away.

Make a **blue** line to put the **blue** crayon away.

Make a **green** line to put the **green** crayon away.

◆ **Finish the sentence.**

_____

_____

My favorite color is _____ .

Peanut Butter

You can eat peanut butter on bread. You can eat it on crackers. You can eat it with jam. I like to eat it on apples.

Peanut butter is made from peanuts and oil. The peanuts are ground up. Then a little oil is added. Now you have peanut butter.

◆ **Answer the questions.**

1. What can we eat with peanut butter?

   _____   _____

   - - - - - - - - - - - - - -   - - - - - - - - - - - - - -

   _____   _____

   _____   _____

   - - - - - - - - - - - - - -   - - - - - - - - - - - - - -

   _____   _____

2. What is peanut butter made from?

   _____   _____

   - - - - - - - - - - - - - -   - - - - - - - - - - - - - -

   _____ and _____

3. How do you like to eat peanut butter?

   _____

   -

   _____

Break the Code!

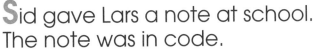

Sid gave Lars a note at school.
The note was in code.
Help Lars break the code.

12-5-20-19   16-12-1-25   19-16-25.

3-15-13-5   15-22-5-18

1-6-20-5-18   19-3-8-15-15-12.

◆ Write the correct letters in the boxes.
Then read the message.

1	2	3	4	5	6	7	8	9	10	11	12	13	14	15	16	17	18	19	20	21	22	23	24	25	26
A	B	C	D	E	F	G	H	I	J	K	L	M	N	O	P	Q	R	S	T	U	V	W	X	Y	Z

12 5 20 19

16 12 1 25

19 16 25

3 15 13 5

15 22 5 18

1 6 20 5 18

19 3 8 15 15 12

Put Things Away

Do you put things away?
That makes them easy to find later.

Lisa puts her toys away.
She puts the art things in the art box.
She puts toys in the toy box.
She puts books in the bookshelf.

◆ **Draw lines from the things to where they go.**

At the Circus

◆ **Color the boxes to show how many.**

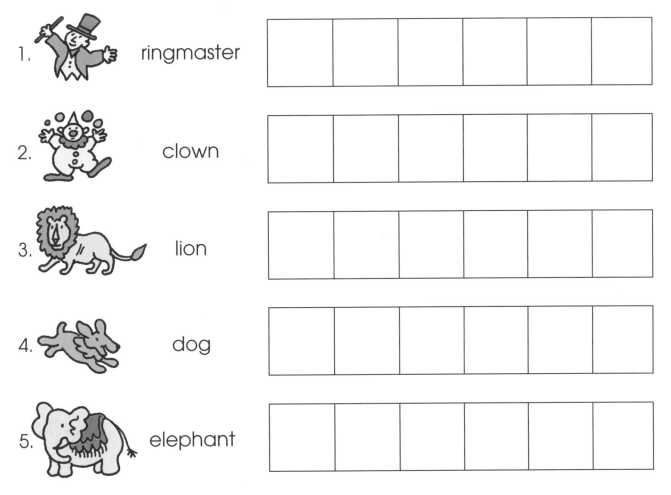

1. ringmaster

2. clown

3. lion

4. dog

5. elephant

Comparison/Picture Clues

Book Covers

A book cover tells the name of the book.
It tells who wrote the book.
It tells who drew the pictures.

MY VALENTINE BOOK
Written by Tyrone James
Pictures by Robert James

◆ **Check the things that a book cover tells.**

1. ☐ who wrote the book   ☐ the name of the book

   ☐ when the book was made   ☐ who drew the pictures

◆ **Answer the questions.**

2. Who wrote this book?

_____

- -

_____

3. Who drew the pictures?

_____

- -

_____

4. What is this book about?

_____

- -

_____

Think Big!

◆ Draw lines to things that are almost the same, but bigger.

1.

2.

3.

4.

5.

6.

◆ **Draw a line from each sentence to the correct picture.**

1. This tool is for digging.

A.

2. This tool is for writing.

B.

3. These tools are for eating.

C.

4. This is for firefighting.

D.

5. These are for running.

E.

6. This is for mailing.

F.

7. This is for the dark.

G.

8. This takes you sailing.

H.

Referents/Picture Clues

Unscramble Puzzle

◆ **Unscramble the clues.**
Use the words in the box.
Write the words in the puzzle.

blue
boat
drum
into
mine
tree

Across ▶

1. lube
3. mudr
5. iton

Down ▼

1. oatb
2. eret
4. nmie

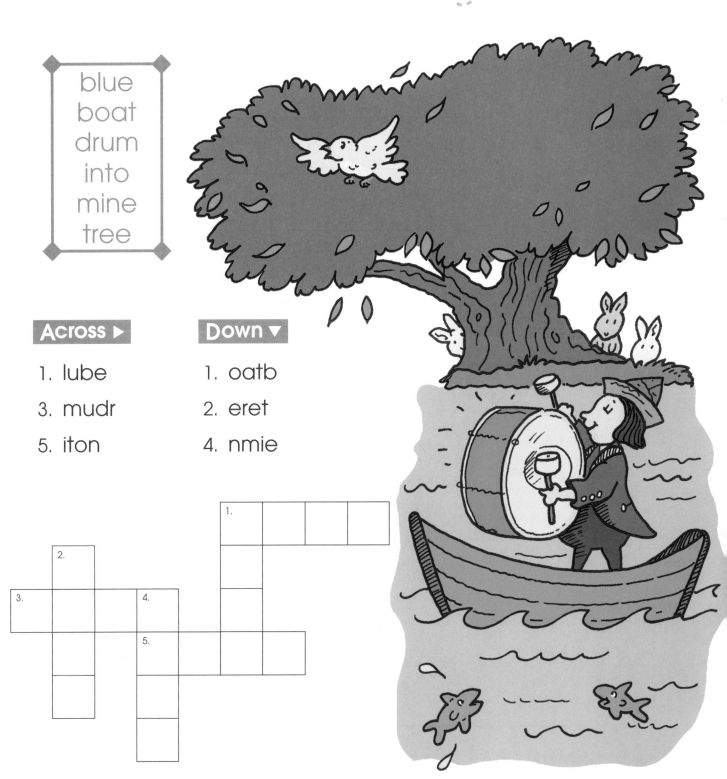

I Can Read and Write!

◆ **Finish the story. Use List A or List B.**
Read your story to a friend.

List A

store

dad

a book

people

List B

circus

mom

a balloon

clowns

_____

_____

Today I will go to the _____ .

_____

_____

My _____ will go with me.

_____

_____

It will be fun! I will buy _____ .

_____

_____

I will see _____ .

I will read the words I see!

254

Context Clues/Picture Clues

Answer Key

Page 225
1. (name)
2. (age)
3. (# of brothers)
4. (# of sisters)
5. read

Drawings will vary.

Page 226
1. 6 swings or 2 swing sets
3. 2 slides
5. Accept swings or benches.
7. seesaws
2. 3 seesaws
4. 3 benches
6. benches
8. Accept swings or seesaws.

Page 227
1. Jenny
2. birthday
3. house
4. May 5
5. 2:00 PM
6. Answers will vary.

Page 228
2 (Pick out a pet.)
3 (Take your pet home.)
1 (Go to a pet store.)
4 (Name your pet.)

Page 229
1. C
2. B
3. A
4. F
5. D
6. E
7. H
8. G

Page 230
1. wagon
3. ring
5. cake or juice
2. car
4. swimsuit
6. blue jeans

Page 231

				¹l	o	s	t
	²g			e			
³c	o	l	⁴d	f			
			⁵o	u	t		
			w				
			n				

Page 232
I like red flowers and purple balloons.

Page 233
Child should add one picture to each group. Answers should be words from one box above.

Page 234
1. 6 tulips   8 lilies   7 balloon flowers
   6 pansies   5 daisies   11 roses
2. rose
3. daisy
4. pansy
5. Answers will vary.

Page 235
4
1
3
2

Page 236
1. bus
2. driver
3. kids
4. no
5. yes
6. school

Page 237
1. C
2. B
3. A
4. E
5. F
6. D
7. H
8. G

Page 238
1. (left) cat drinking
2. (right) dog jumping
3. (left) macaw on branch
4. (left) shark in water

Answer Key

Answer Key

Page 239

	¹c	l	o	s	e	²d	
	o			²p		r	
⁴h	l	³d		e		y	
⁵o	l	d		⁶n	e	w	
	t						

Page 240

1. Sara
2. Kenji
3. Mia
4. Ty
5. Mimi
6. Bob

Page 241

1. near a wall
2. 10 steps away
3. toss it
4. in a hole
5. 10 pennies

Page 242

1. (right) silly man
2. (left) green car
3. (right) magician's hat
4. (left) silly pet

Page 243

1. child swimming
2. child skating
3. child eating
4. snowman melted

Page 244

bird
pin
boy
bow

Page 245

Child should use the color of each crayon to draw the line to the box.

Answers will vary.

Page 246

1. bread
   crackers
   jam
   apples
2. peanuts, oil
3. Answers will vary.

Page 247

Let's play spy. Come over after school.

Page 248

books to bookshelf
toys to toy box
art supplies to art box

Page 249

ringmaster (1 box colored)
clown (4 boxes colored)
lion (3 boxes colored)
dog (5 boxes colored)
elephant (3 boxes colored)

Page 250

1. who wrote the book
   the name of the book
   who drew the pictures
2. Tyrone James
3. Robert James
4. valentines

Page 251

1. bowl—pool
2. blocks—skyscraper
3. broccoli—forest
4. name tag—city sign
5. potatoes—mountains
6. faucet—waterfall

Page 252

1. B
2. C
3. D
4. A
5. H
6. E
7. F
8. G

Page 253

					¹b	l	u	e
	²t				o			
³d	r	u	m	⁴m		a		
	e			⁵i	n	t	o	
	e			n				
				e				

Page 254

Answers will vary.
Story should make sense.

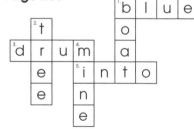

Answer Key

Jump Rope Chant

A-B-C-D and E-F-G
I knew that when I was three.

H-I-J-K and L-M-N-O-P
Q-R-S and T-U-V
Letters make the words I see.

W-X and Y and Z
The alphabet is fun for me!

◆ **Circle the right answer.**

1. What is the poem about?

   seeing the sun   lunch time

   three toys   the alphabet

2. What is the best name for the poem?

   Letter Fun   Happy Birthday

   Time to Play   Going to School

3. What makes the words we see?

   houses   trees

   letters   me

4. What does the poem say the alphabet is?

   nice   fun

   easy   hard

Cooking Fish

Cookie is a cat. Cookie likes cooking. Cookie cooks what he likes to eat.

Cookie cooks cake. He cooks it from fish. Cookie cooks pie from fish too. Cookie even cooks cookies from fish!

◆ **Circle the right answer.**

1. What is the best name for the story?

   Real Cats   Eating Cookies   A Cat That Cooks

2. What does Cookie use to make everything he cooks?

   cookies   pie   fish   cake

3. What kind of animal is Cookie?

   a real cow   a make-believe cow

   a real cat   a make-believe cat

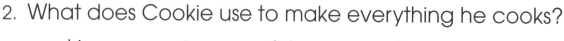

◆ **Circle yes or no to show which sentences are right.**

4. Real cats can cook   yes   no
5. Real cats like to eat fish.   yes   no
6. Cookie is a real cat.   yes   no

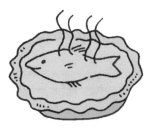
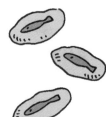

Scary Night

It was dark. It was night. Tina heard something go "Whoooo!" Tina was scared. Then, Tina heard something go "Whoooo!" again.

The window blew open. She went to close it. She saw an owl and it said, "Whoooo!" Tina was happy again.

◆ **Circle the right answer.**

1. What is the story about?

   falling asleep   reading a book

   how owls live   a scary night

2. What is the best name for the story?

   A Scary Sound   Tina's Closet

   Waking Up!   Tina's Pet

3. What did Tina hear?

   an open window   her mom

   a ghost   an owl

◆ **Write 1,2,3 to show how things happened.**

4. _____ The window blew open.

5. _____ Tina heard something go "Whoooo!"

6. _____ Tina saw an owl.

A Note

> Mom,
>
> I am outside. I went to
> the park. Adam is with me.
> We will be home by noon.
>
> I love you,
> Erica

◆ **Circle the right answer.**

1. What kind of writing is this?

   a funny story   a report card

   a sign   a note

2. Did Mom write the note?   yes   no
3. Did Erica write the note?   yes   no
4. Is the note to Adam?   yes   no
5. Is the note to Mom?   yes   no
6. Is Erica going to the park?   yes   no
7. Is Adam going to the park?   yes   no
8. Will Erica be home by noon?   yes   no

9. Who do you think Adam is?

   Erica's dad   Erica's teacher

   Erica's friend   Erica's goldfish

Apples

There are many kinds of apples. Apples are red. Apples are yellow. Apples are green. All apples grow on trees.

Some apples are sweet. Sweet apples taste best raw. Other apples are tart. Tart apples taste best cooked.

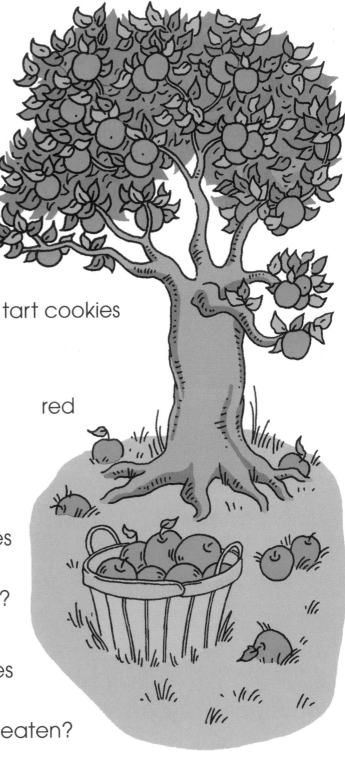

◆ **Circle the right answer.**

1. What is the story about?

   sweet things   apples   tart cookies

2. What does **tart** mean?

   sweet   yellow   sour   red

3. Which apples taste best raw?

   sweet apples   red apples

   tart apples   green apples

4. Which apples taste best cooked?

   sweet apples   red apples

   tart apples   green apples

5. Which kinds of apples have you eaten?

Kids' Work . . .

Would you like a job? There are many jobs for kids. Kids can rake leaves. They can sweep sidewalks. Kids can help carry packages too.

But kids cannot drive. So there are some jobs kids cannot do now. They must wait to drive a taxi. They must wait to drive a dump truck.

◆ **Answer the questions.**

1. What is the best name for the story?

   Being a Driver   Helping Mom

   Jobs for Kids   Kids Are Too Little

2. What is something kids cannot do?

   rake leaves   sweep sidewalks

   carry packages   drive a car

3. What must kids do before they can drive?

   rake   sweep

   wait   carry

4. What work will you do when you grow up?

   _____

   -

   _____

The Party . . . . . .

The monsters had a party. They played monster games. They did monster dances. Then they cleaned up.

A monster mom looked in. She said, "Be good! Monsters are messy. Mess this room up, right now!"

◆ **Circle the right answer.**

1. Which one is a **monster**?

2. What is the best name for the story?

A Monster Party   Very Mean Monsters

Real Monsters   Monster Foods

3. What did the monster mom want the monsters to do?

clean up   be quiet

make a mess   go to sleep

◆ **Draw a line to the word that is the opposite.**

4. clean   worked

5. played   messy

Baseball Cheer

Our team is the best.
Our team never rests.

Our team really hits.
Our team never quits.

Before the games begin
We know that we will win!

Our team never rests.
Our team is the best!

◆ **Circle the right answer.**

1. What is the poem about?

    our family   our baseball team

    our school   our church

2. What is a **team**?

    a group working together to win

    a group working together to lose

3. What does our team never do?

    win   lose

    quit   hit

4. What do we know before the game?

    We will lose.   We will rest.

    We will quit.   We will win.

Leaf Mystery

The wind was blowing. Leaves fell from the trees. Many leaves were red, orange and yellow. Ty found a red leaf.

"This leaf is not real," said Ty. "Leaves are green."

But the leaf was real. What season was it?

◆ **Circle the right answer.**

1. What is the best name for the story?

   The Winter   The Red Leaf   Ty's Ride

2. Which picture shows the weather that day?

3. What did Ty find?

4. What season was it?

   spring   summer   fall

The Alien

Hal didn't like being an alien. He wanted to be a kid. He left home. He went to Earth.

Hal saw a doll by a tree. He thought it was a kid. So Hal stood very still. It was not fun.

Hal was an alien. He went back home. His mom was glad he did.

◆ **Circle the right answer.**

1. What is the story about?

   a doll   an alien   Earth

2. What is an **alien**?

   someone from another planet

   a kid who wants to be doll

3. What did Hal want to be?

   a doll   a kid   a tree

4. Which one do you think is Hal?

Scary Sunday

When Zach got up, no one was home. Where was his family? He heard a whine. It was scary.

The car was in the driveway. There was no note. He heard nothing but that whine.

They were out back! "Happy Birthday!" the family said. They were playing with Zach's new puppy!

◆ Circle the right answer.

1. What is the best name for the story?

   My First Birthday   Zach's Surprise   The Family Car

2. What did Zach hear?

   the family car   a note

   his family   a whine

◆ Draw a line to the end of each sentence.

3. When Zach woke up   a whine.

4. He heard   was in the driveway.

5. The car   no one was home.

6. "Happy Birthday!"   with Zach's new puppy.

7. They were playing   the family said.

A Thank You

Dear Grandma,

You sent such a nice surprise! Thank you for my new skates. They will look great with my new helmet. Raul says they are the best skates he's ever seen!

I love you,
Maria

◆ **Circle the right answer.**

1. What kind of writing is this?

   a note   a song

   a birthday card   a book

2. Who wrote it?

   Maria   Grandma   Mom

3. Who is it for?

   Grandma   Raul   no one

4. What will Maria wear with her skates?

Clothes

People all over the world wear clothes. Clothes keep us warm. Clothes protect us from the sun.

Some clothes are uniforms. Uniforms are special clothes. They tell us about a person's job. What uniforms do you see in your town?

◆ **Circle the right answer.**

1. What is the story about?

   the sun   people   clothes   the world

2. Which one is a uniform?

3. What is one way clothes help us?

   They are too big.   They keep us warm.

   They are many colors.   They are called uniforms.

4. What do uniforms tell us?

   special clothes   a person's job

   keep us warm   someone's address

Working Dogs

Have you seen a working dog? In Alaska, dogs pull sleds over the snow. Dogsleds work better than cars in the snow.

Working dogs help people who cannot see. The dog leads the way when the owner walks outside. The dog helps the owner know where to go.

◆ **Circle the right answer.**

1. What is the story about?

    pet dogs   working dogs

    Alaska   people who cannot see

2. What work do some dogs do?

    drive a car   pull a sled   sleep

3. What other work do some dogs do?

    help people eat   help people sleep

    help people who cannot see   help people dance

4. Do dogs pull sleds?   yes   no

5. Do dogs drive cars?   yes   no

6. Do dogs help people eat?   yes   no

7. Do dogsleds work better   yes   no
   than cars in the snow?

The Dance

It would be the best dance!
Every dinosaur was coming.
Deeny wanted to be cool.
He got out his cool dino shoes.

Uh-oh! One shoe had a hole!
Deeny filled the hole with gum.
When the music began, Deeny
stuck to the floor! So he took off
his shoes. He was cool anyway.

◆ Circle the right answer.

1. What is the best name for the story?

   Deeny's Mom   Good Music

   Real Dinosaurs   Deeny's Dancing Shoes

2. What did Deeny put in his shoe?

   a dance   gum   a hole

3. What happened when Deeny started to dance?

   He put on his shoes.   He fell down.

   He stuck to the floor.   He was not cool.

4. Which one is Deeny?

A Rhyme

There was an old woman
who lived in a boot.
She fed all her children
on crackers and fruit.

When nighttime would come,
she'd say, "Off to bed! Scoot!"
And she'd play them to sleep
with a song from her flute.

◆ **Circle the right answer.**

1. What is the poem about?

   a real family   an ant family

   boots   music

2. What does **scoot** mean?

   go quickly   go slowly

3. What does the woman make with her flute?

   boots   music

   crackers   beds

◆ **Circle each picture that rhymes with scoot.**

Round Riddle

You see me at the beach. You see me in a game. I am round and filled with air. Sometimes I can bounce.

Some people use me to float. Some people use me to play catch. Some people try to sit on me! What am I?

◆ **Circle the right answer.**

1. What kind of writing is this?

   note   riddle   sign

2. What is the best name for the riddle?

   Sandy Places   Games and Work

   What Am I?   Playing in the Rain

3. What is the riddle about?

   a swimsuit   a towel

   a beach ball   a float

◆ **Circle yes or no about each sentence.**

4. It can bounce.   yes   no

5. It is always red.   yes   no

6. It is round.   yes   no

7. It can float.   yes   no

The Bug

Willie was a little car. But everyone called him "The Bug." He couldn't go fast. But he was always ready.

One day when the family had a problem, they got in their fast car. It didn't work. But Willie was ready. Willie saved the day!

◆ **Circle the right answer.**

1. What is the story about?

   a family   a car   a bug

2. What is the best name for the story?

   My Family   Willie Saves the Day

   Fast Cars Are Best   How I Broke My Arm

3. What was it that Willie could not do?

   go slow   be ready

   go fast   smile

4. Which one do you think is Willie?

Whose Footprints?

One day, Mia saw footprints in her yard. Mia's mom was inside. Dad was inside too. Whose footprints were they? Was a robber coming?

Mia watched. No one came. She got scared. She told her parents. They smiled at her! "Mia, those are your footprints!" they said.

◆ Circle the right answer.

1. What is the story about?

   playing in the yard   finding footprints

   staying inside   smiling and talking

2. Who did Mia think made the footprints?

   Mia's dad   a robber   Mia's mom

3. Who really made the footprints?

   Mia   Mia's mom   a robber

◆ Draw lines to match the footprint with the one who made it.

4.

5.

An Invitation

Dear Jeremy,

We're having a party on the 4th of July. We can watch fireworks! Will you come? There will be a picnic at 6:00. Bring foods you like to eat.

See you there,
Tyrone

◆ **Circle the right answer.**

1. What kind of writing is this?

   an invitation   a song   a book

2. What kind of party is it?

   a skating party   a picnic   a birthday party

3. What should Jeremy bring?

  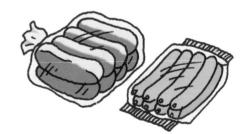

4. Is the party for Thanksgiving?   yes   no
5. Is the party for the Fourth of July?   yes   no
6. Does the party start at 6:00?   yes   no
7. Will there be food at the party?   yes   no

Friends

Friends are people who care about you. They want you to be happy. They like to be with you.

Friends are special people who share your feelings. Friends make the world a better place.

◆ **Circle the right answer.**

1. What is the story about?

   places   friends

   feelings   the world

2. What is one thing friends do?

   They make the world bad.   They do not care.

   They share your feelings.   They want you to be unhappy.

◆ **Draw a line to the end of each sentence.**

3. Friends are people   to be happy.

4. They want you   special people.

5. They like to   who care about you.

6. Friends are   be with you.

7. Friends make the world   a better place.

The Library . . . . .

Sshh...You are in a library. People read in the library. So please be quiet.

When you are here in the library, you can pick out a book. You can take the book home to read it. But remember to bring it back!

◆ **Circle the right answer.**

1. What is the story about?

   people   real things

   the library   storybooks

2. What can you do at the library?

   pick out a book   watch a show

   eat lunch   make noise

3. What should you remember to do with your book?

   be quiet   bring it back   give it away

◆ **Write 1,2,3 to show the right order.**

4. _____ Take the book home.

5. _____ Pick out a book.

6. _____ Bring it back to the library.

Mouse's House

Mouse needed a house. It did not have to be big. It did not have to be pretty. It had to be dry. It had to be warm, because winter was coming.

Mouse looked in a tree. It was not warm. Mouse looked under a leaf. It was not dry. Mouse found a boot. Mouse had a new home!

◆ **Circle the right answer.**

1. What is the story about?

   snow in winter   climbing a tree

   finding a house   Mouse's family

2. What did the house have to be?

   warm and pretty   big and dry

   warm and dry   big and pretty

3. Why did Mouse need a house?

   Trees are cold.   His house burned down.

   He was lost.   Winter was coming.

4. Which do you think is Mouse's new house?

Real and Make-Believe

Monkey Poem

Five little monkeys went to play
Out in the park one sunny day.

When Uncle Baboon said,
"On your way!"
All the little monkeys said,
"Can we stay?"

So Uncle Baboon said, "Oh, okay!
I do like to see my monkeys play."

◆ **Circle the right answer.**

1. What is the best name for the poem?

   Monkeys in the Park   The Mad Baboon

2. Who was the baboon?

   the monkeys' dad   the monkeys' uncle   the park owner

3. Was only one monkey playing?   yes   no
4. Was the baboon their mom?   yes   no
5. Did the monkeys want to stay?   yes   no
6. Did the baboon ask them to go?   yes   no
7. Did the baboon let them stay?   yes   no

Mystery Man

The stranger walked into the barn.
He was wearing a long coat and
a hat. He had hair on his chin.
He did not talk. Who was he?

Cow was afraid. Horse was afraid.
Rat went up to take a closer look.
The stranger's legs were hairy.
He had a tail. It was just Goat.
Goat was playing a trick!

◆ **Circle the right answer.**

1. What is the best name for the story?

   The Animals   On the Farm

   Stranger in the Barn   Rat Games

2. What did the stranger wear?

   a coat and shoes   a hat and coat

   a hat and pants   pants and shoes

3. Who was in the coat?

   Cow   Rat

   Horse   Goat

4. What was Goat doing?

   playing a trick   showing off his coat

   going to school   trying to hide

Sid

Sid, a snake, likes to make shapes. Sid makes a circle when he sees the sun. Sid makes an S when someone asks his name. Sid makes an egg when he sees a bird.

But Sid is too curvy. He never can make a triangle. He never can make a square.

◆ **Circle the right answer.**

1. What is the best name for the story?

   Real Snakes   The Sun   Sid's Shapes

2. What did Sid like to make?

   shapes   breakfast   a square

3. Sid could make a circle.   yes   no
4. Sid could make a triangle.   yes   no
5. Sid could make an S.   yes   no

◆ **Draw a picture of Sid in the box below.**

School Mystery

Jess got dressed, the same as every day. She put on her clothes. She put on her shoes. Jess ate her breakfast. She kissed Mom and walked to school.

No one was there! The rooms were empty. The doors were locked. "Goodness," thought Jess. "It's Saturday!"

◆ **Circle the right answer.**

1. What is the best name for the story?

   Jess Goes to School   Jess Sleeps Late

   Go to the Store   A New Home

2. Where did Jess go?

   to her house   to Grandma's   to school

3. How did Jess get there?

A Sign

Welcome to the Park!
The park is open from 9:00 to 5:00

Come see the show!
Shows are at 10:00 and 2:00.
Rules:
Do not feed the animals.
Do not litter.
Do not pick the wildflowers.
DO HAVE FUN!

◆ **Circle the right answer.**

1. What kind of writing is this?

   a sign   a song   a book

2. Where would you find this?

   at school   in the park   in church

3. When does the show start?

   10:00 and 9:00   9:00 and 5:00   10:00 and 2:00

4. What is okay for you to do at the park?

Our Flag

This is our American flag. Some people call our flag "The Stars and Stripes."

Our flag is red, white and blue. Our flag has 13 stripes. There are 7 red stripes. There are 6 white stripes. There are 50 stars. There is one star for each state in our country.

◆ **Circle the right answer.**

1. What is the story about?

   the flag   colors

   stars   stripes

2. What color are the stripes?

   50 red, 13 white   7 red, 6 white

   6 red, 7 white   13 red, 50 white

3. Why are there 50 stars?

   There are 50 states.   The stars are very small.

   There are 50 stripes too.   There are 50 stars in the sky.

4. What do some people call our flag?

   The Red and White   The Strips and Stripes

   The Stars and Stripes   The Red and Blue

The Artist

Pete is a polar bear. Pete is an artist. But everything Pete draws looks like Pete.

Pete painted a house. It was big, white and furry. Pete painted the door. It had sharp, pointy teeth. Pete painted a garden, but the flowers looked like claws. Silly Pete!

◆ **Circle the right answer.**

1. What is the best name for the story?

   Pete's Garden   Real Polar Bears   Pete the Artist

2. Is Pete a person?   yes   no

3. Is Pete a bear?   yes   no

4. Does Pete have claws?   yes   no

5. Is Pete little?   yes   no

◆ **Draw a picture Pete might draw.**

Answer Key

Page 257
1. the alphabet
2. Letter Fun
3. letters
4. fun

Page 258
1. A Cat That Cooks
2. fish
3. a make-believe cat
4. no
5. yes
6. no

Page 259
1. a scary night
2. A Scary Sound
3. an owl
4. 2
5. 1
6. 3

Page 260
1. a note
2. no
3. yes
4. no
5. yes
6. yes
7. yes
8. yes
9. Erica's friend

Page 261
1. apples
2. sour
3. sweet apples
4. tart apples
5. Answers will vary.

Page 262
1. Jobs for Kids
2. drive a car
3. wait
4. Answers will vary.

Page 263
1. monster picture
2. A Monster Party
3. make a mess
4. messy
5. worked

Page 264
1. our baseball team
2. a group working together to win
3. quit
4. We will win.

Page 265
1. The Red Leaf
2. windy picture
3. red leaf picture
4. fall

Page 266
1. an alien
2. someone from another planet
3. a kid
4. alien picture

Page 267
1. Zach's Surprise
2. a whine
3. no one was home.
4. a whine.
5. was in the driveway.
6. the family said.
7. with Zach's new puppy.

Page 268
1. a note
2. Maria
3. Grandma
4. helmet picture

Page 269
1. clothes
2. uniform picture
3. They keep us warm.
4. a person's job

Page 270
1. working dogs
2. pull a sled
3. help people who cannot see
4. yes
5. no
6. no
7. yes

Page 271
1. Deeny's Dancing Shoes
2. gum
3. He stuck to the floor.
4. yellow dinosaur picture

Answer Key

Page 272
1. an ant family
2. go quickly
3. music
4. boot picture and fruit picture

Page 273
1. riddle
2. What Am I?
3. a beach ball
4. yes
5. no
6. yes
7. yes

Page 274
1. a car
2. Willie Saves the Day
3. go fast
4. yellow car picture

Page 275
1. finding footprints
2. a robber
3. Mia
4. dog
5. Mia

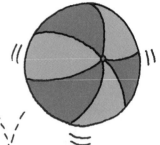

Page 276
1. an invitation
2. a picnic
3. food picture
4. no
5. yes
6. yes
7. yes

Page 277
1. friends
2. They share your feelings.
3. who care about you.
4. to be happy.
5. be with you.
6. special people.
7. a better place.

Page 278
1. the library
2. pick out a book
3. bring it back
4. 2
5. 1
6. 3

Page 279
1. finding a house
2. warm and dry
3. Winter was coming.
4. boot picture

Page 280
1. Monkeys in the Park
2. the monkeys' uncle
3. no
4. no
5. yes
6. yes
7. yes

Page 281
1. Stranger in the Barn
2. a hat and coat
3. Goat
4. playing a trick

Page 282
1. Sid's Shapes
2. shapes
3. yes
4. no
5. yes
   Answers will vary, but should show a snake.

Page 283
1. Jess Goes to School
2. to school
3. picture of walking

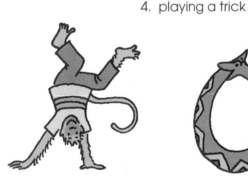

Page 284
1. a sign
2. in the park
3. 10:00 and 2:00
4. picture of a child and Dad playing ball

Page 285
1. the flag
2. 7 red, 6 white
3. There are 50 states.
4. The Stars and Stripes

Page 286
1. Pete the Artist
2. no
3. yes
4. yes
5. no
   Answers will vary, but should look like something Pete would draw.

A Cheer for Me!

I can read a book.
I can learn to cook.
I can count to 103.

I can walk with a wiggle
That makes you giggle,
Or buzz like a bumblebee.

It will always be true
That I am not just like you,
But I make a wonderful me!

◆ **Circle the right answer.**

1. What is the best name for the poem?

   I'm the Best Me!   I Am Better Than You

   I Can Buzz   I Am Pretty

2. Which word rhymes with **giggle**?

   make   wiggle   bumblebee

3. What does **wonderful** mean?

   bad   really great   silly

◆ **Unscramble the word to answer the question.**

4. What does a bumblebee do?

   _____

   _ _ _ _ _ _ _ _ _ _ _ _ _ _ _ _ _ _

   zubz _____

Bone Mystery

Dog likes to make things. When he is at work, Dog often does things without thinking.

Yesterday Dog made a table. He planned to sit at it and write letters to his friends. When the table was done, he wanted to chew on a big bone. But all four of his bones were gone! Can you find Dog's bones?

◆ **Circle the right answer.**

1. What is the best name for the story?

   My Bones Are Missing!   Dog Makes Bones

   Bones Are Good for Dogs   Dog Works Hard

2. What will Dog do at his new table?

   chew bones   make things   write letters

3. What happened to Dog's bones?

   They were stolen.   They were thrown out.   Dog used them.

4. What does **do things without thinking** mean?

   not think about what you do   chew on a nice big bone

5. Which things were named in the story?

Drawing Conclusions

Computer Cat

Computer Cat is a whiz on her computer. She can make drawings with her mouse. She can write long letters with the keys. She can write stories too.

Computer Cat is writing a book. The book is about using a Cat Computer. She will sell her book on TV! Would you buy it?

◆ Circle the right answer.

1. What is the story about?

   a cat who writes and draws   a cat and a mouse

   a computer mouse   a book about TV

2. Does Computer Cat draw pictures?   yes   no

3. Does Computer Cat chase her mouse?   yes   no

4. Does Computer Cat write letters?   yes   no

5. Which cat is Computer Cat?

Scary Nightmare

Henry was sleeping. He dreamed he was being chased. A lion wanted to eat him!

The lion was red. Then it was blue. Then it was yellow. The jungle changed color too. But the lion's teeth were always white.

Finally Henry woke up. He was glad the dream was over!

◆ **Circle the right answer.**

1. What is the best name for the story?

   Real Lions   Make-Believe Lions

   Henry's Dream   A Scary Day

2. What did Henry dream about?

   a lion chasing him   rainbows in the sky   going to bed

3. Where were Henry and the lion together?

   in bed   in the jungle   on a rainbow

4. What is a **nightmare**?

   a bad dream   a lion   teeth

◆ **Draw a line to the end of each sentence.**

5. The lion   were always white.

6. The lion's teeth   was red.

7. The jungle   changed color too.

Will You Play?

Jackie,

Will you play on our team? You are great at basketball. You're a super shooter. We need players who can score.

We practice on Tuesdays at 7:00. Games are on Saturdays. Please come play with us!

Your friend,
Kris

◆ **Circle the right answer.**

1. What kind of writing is this?

   a funny story   a sign   a note

2. Who wrote it?

   Kris   Mom   Erica

3. Who is Kris?

   Jackie's aunt   Jackie's sister   Jackie's friend

4. What does Jackie do well?

   run   pass   shoot

5. When does the team practice?

   Tuesdays   Saturdays   every day

6. What does **super** mean?

   very good   very bad   very slow

Dinosaur Bones

We know about dinosaurs from their bones. People hunt for dinosaur bones all over the world. They look in places where other bones were found.

Their bones can tell us how big dinosaurs were. Bones can tell us what shape they were. But bones cannot tell us what color dinosaurs were. Nobody knows that for sure.

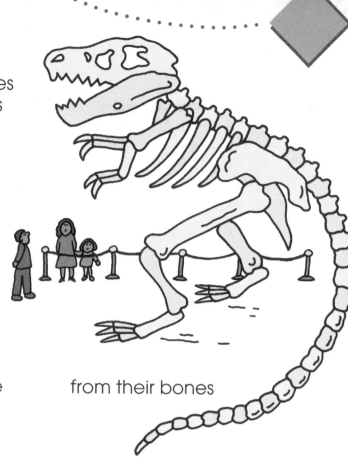

◆ **Circle the right answer.**

1. How do we know about dinosaurs?

   from their size   from their shape   from their bones

2. What do dinosaur bones tell us?

   what size they were   what color they were   what they ate

3. What do the bones not tell us?

   their shape   their size   their color

4. Where do people look for bones?

   in backyards   all over the world   in the sea

5. Which dinosaur would have the largest bones?

Recalling Ideas

A Fun Phone!

Make a simple telephone. It's easy to do. You need two clean paper cups and a long piece of string.

Put a hole in the bottom of each cup. Push the string through the holes. Tie knots in the ends of the string. Make the knots on the inside of each cup.

Put one cup to your ear. Have a friend talk in the other cup. What do you hear?

◆ Circle the right answer.

1. What is the best name for the story?

   Make a TV   Make a Telephone

   Colorful String   Two Fancy Cups

2. What can you make with two cups and some string?

   a telephone   a television   a telescope

3. Where do you put a hole?

   in the bottom of one cup   in the bottom of both cups

4. Where do you tie a knot?

   in one end of the string   in both ends of the string

◆ Write what you would say to your friend on the telephone.

_____

_____

_____

No Cookies!

Every day Bear came to my door. Every day he asked for a cookie. He did not want cake. He did not want ice cream. He wanted just cookies.

I always said "Not today. Not ever. Bears do not eat cookies!"

One day Bear came to my door. He gave me a present. It was a giant bag of cookies. Bear said, "May I have a cookie, please?"

What could I do? I said, "Sure."

◆ **Circle the right answer.**

1. How often did the bear come?

   once a week   every day   one day

2. What did the bear bring one day?

   cookies   cake   ice cream

3. What does **giant** mean?

   very small   very old   very big

◆ **Write the word to finish each sentence.**

4. Every day, Bear came to my _____ .

5. "May I have a cookie, _____ ?"

Ben's Robot

Ben had a robot
who never forgot
anything Ben ever told him.

Sometimes the robot would do
what Ben told him not to.
Then Ben would quietly scold him.

◆ **Circle the right answer.**

1. What is the best name for the poem?

    Ben Plays   Bad Robot!   Bad Ben!   The Robot Forgets

2. What does the robot never do?

    forget   anything   talk

3. What does the robot never forget?

    what he sees   what Ben tells him

4. What does **scold** mean?

    to say you did something wrong   to say you did something right

5. How did the robot get in trouble?

    by doing what Ben said   by doing what Ben said not to do

◆ **Draw a line to the word that rhymes.**

6. told   forgot

7. robot   to

8. do   scold

The Award

The city gave an award today. The award is for the school that reads the most books. Lincoln School won.

The children at Lincoln School will pick out new books. The books go in the school library. Now the children can keep reading.

◆ **Circle the right answer.**

1. Where might you find this writing?

   in a birthday card   in a note to school   in a newspaper

2. What is the best name for the story?

   Lincoln School Wins   The City Is Nice   Awards Are Good

3. What did the children at Lincoln School do?

   read books   made art   wrote stories

4. What does **award** mean?

   a book   a day off   a prize

◆ **Write the title of a book you read. Write what the story was about.**

_____

_____

_____

_____

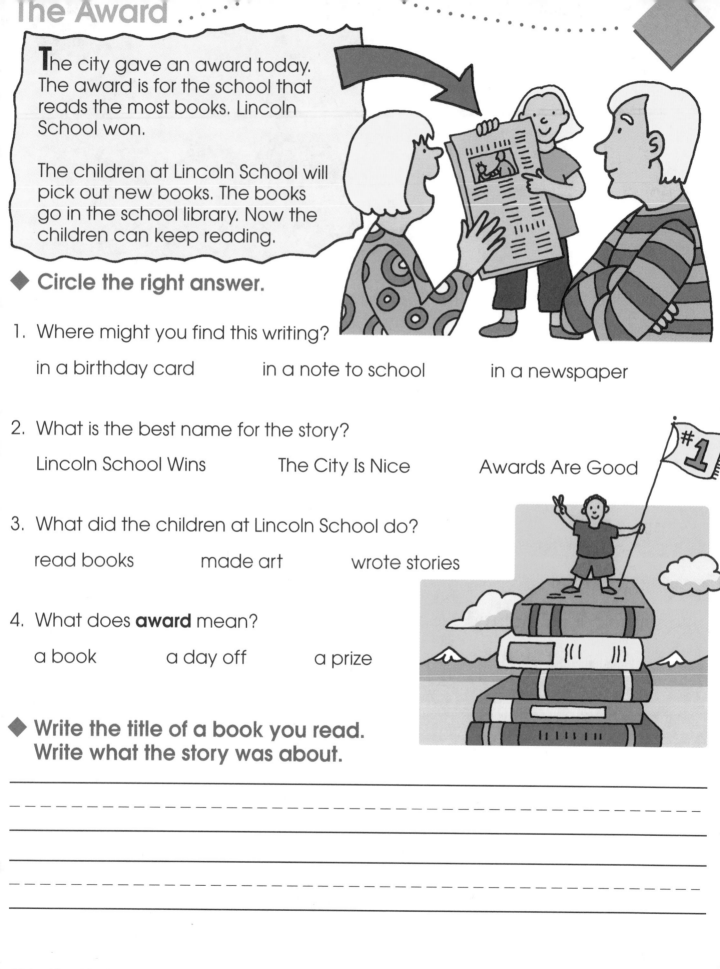

Squirmy Slime

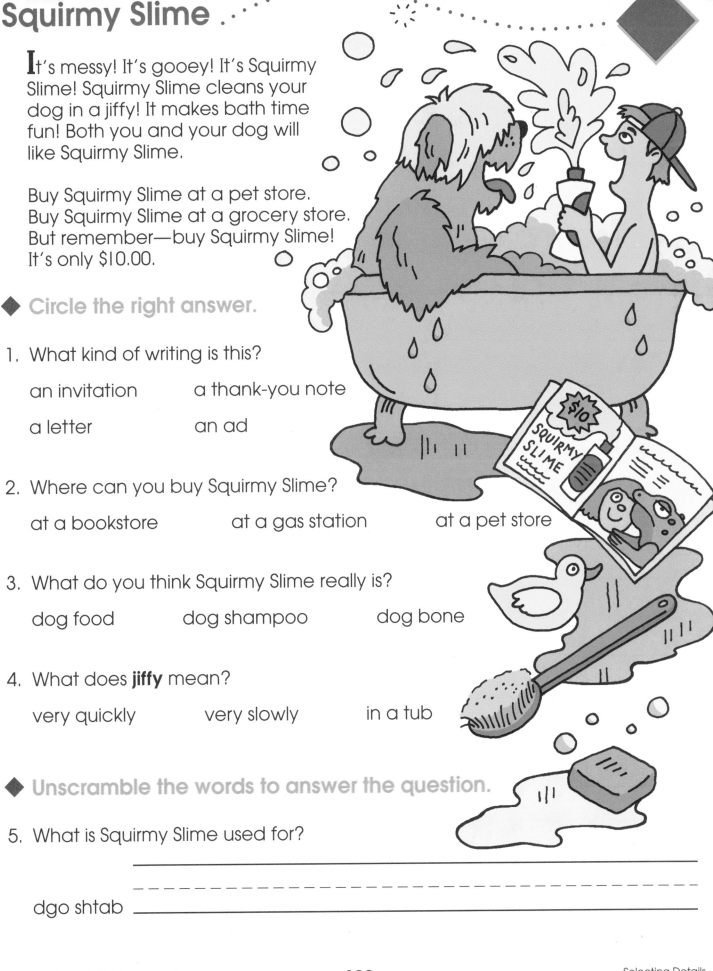

It's messy! It's gooey! It's Squirmy Slime! Squirmy Slime cleans your dog in a jiffy! It makes bath time fun! Both you and your dog will like Squirmy Slime.

Buy Squirmy Slime at a pet store. Buy Squirmy Slime at a grocery store. But remember—buy Squirmy Slime! It's only $10.00.

◆ **Circle the right answer.**

1. What kind of writing is this?

   an invitation   a thank-you note

   a letter   an ad

2. Where can you buy Squirmy Slime?

   at a bookstore   at a gas station   at a pet store

3. What do you think Squirmy Slime really is?

   dog food   dog shampoo   dog bone

4. What does **jiffy** mean?

   very quickly   very slowly   in a tub

◆ **Unscramble the words to answer the question.**

5. What is Squirmy Slime used for?

   _____

   _

   dgo shtab _____

Scary Soup

Grandma was making soup for lunch. Eric told Andy that it was snake soup. He used the ladle to show her a snake. Andy did not like it one bit!

At lunch, Andy told Grandma she would not eat snakes! Grandma just laughed.

"Oh, Andy!" she said. "Don't call them snakes. Those are just noodles!"

◆ **Circle the right answer.**

1. What is the best name for the story?

   Snake Soup   Eric's Dream   Grandma Frowns

2. What kind of soup was really in the pan?

   snake soup   tomato soup   noodle soup

3. What does **bit** mean?

   a snake   a little   a lot

4. What did Eric say was in the soup?

5. Who was cooking lunch?

6. Which is a **ladle**?

Plant a Tree

Dear Neighbors,

Will you help us keep the earth green?
We want to plant trees in our neighborhood.
We want a new tree in every yard.
May we plant one in yours?

We will be planting next week. You can pick
an oak tree, an elm tree or a maple tree.
The trees are free.

The Tree Club

◆ **Circle the right answer.**

1. What kind of writing is this?

   a funny story   a note   a birthday card

2. When is the Tree Club planting trees?

   last week   this week   next week

3. What kind of trees do they have?

   oak, maple, ash   elm, ash, maple   maple, oak, elm

4. What will the trees do for the earth?

   keep it green   put one in your yard   trees are free

5. Which picture shows the Tree Club?

Sport Fun! · · · · · ·

Which sport is best? Miss Miller's class voted for a sport. Each child put up a sticker to show which sport is best.

There were 4 stickers from which to choose. Helmets were for football. Hats were for baseball. Fins were for swimming. Shoes were for running.

Can you tell which sport won? Is that what you would pick?

WHICH SPORT IS BEST?

football | baseball | swimming | running

◆ **Circle the right answer.**

1. Which sticker is for running?

2. What does **voted** mean?

   chose the one you wanted   chose the one you didn't want

3. Which sport won in Miss Miller's class vote?

   football   baseball   running

◆ **Draw the sticker you would choose.**

Giraffe Story

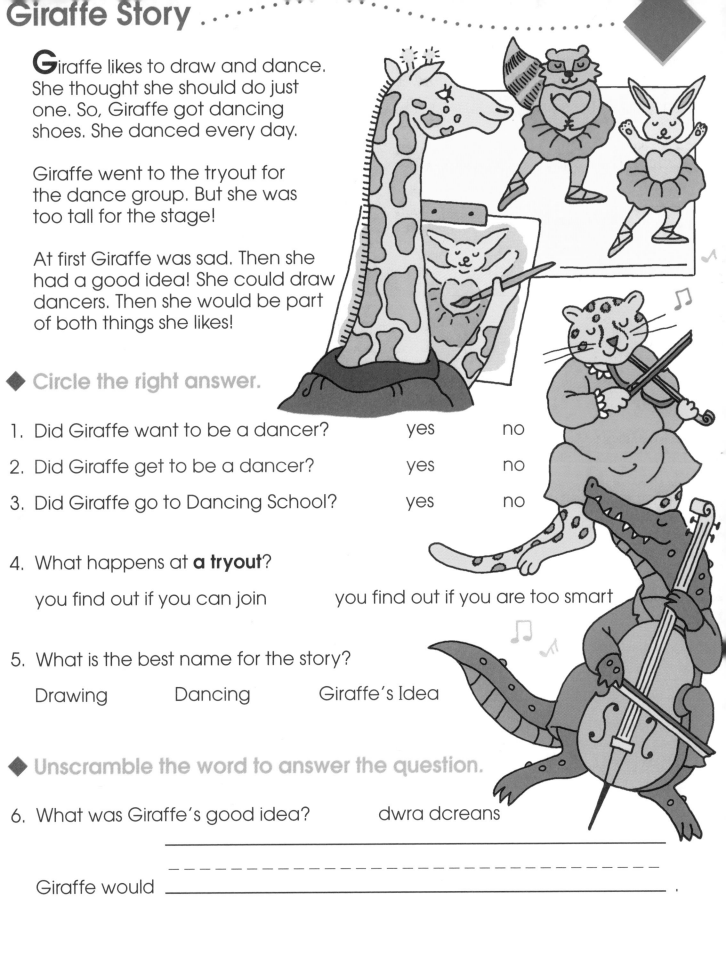

Giraffe likes to draw and dance. She thought she should do just one. So, Giraffe got dancing shoes. She danced every day.

Giraffe went to the tryout for the dance group. But she was too tall for the stage!

At first Giraffe was sad. Then she had a good idea! She could draw dancers. Then she would be part of both things she likes!

◆ Circle the right answer.

1. Did Giraffe want to be a dancer?   yes   no

2. Did Giraffe get to be a dancer?   yes   no

3. Did Giraffe go to Dancing School?   yes   no

4. What happens at **a tryout**?

   you find out if you can join   you find out if you are too smart

5. What is the best name for the story?

   Drawing   Dancing   Giraffe's Idea

◆ Unscramble the word to answer the question.

6. What was Giraffe's good idea?   dwra dcreans

   _____

   _____

   Giraffe would _____ .

Night Poem

The moon tonight
is full and bright.
The stars are shining high.

A falling star flies
before my eyes.
I make a wish as it goes by.

The darkness creeps,
but it's time to sleep.
I say "Goodnight" to the sky.

◆ **Circle the right answer.**

1. What is the best name for the poem?

   The Moon   Goodnight Sky   Darkness

2. What is not named in the poem?

   the stars   the sun   a falling star

3. Which word rhymes with **tonight**?

   high   sky   bright

4. What is full and bright?

   the moon   the stars   darkness

◆ **Circle the missing word.**

5. _____ means **move slowly**.   Creeps   Bright

6. _____ means **goes through the air**.   Sleep   Flies

Reward!

LOST DOG

We lost our black dog!
He was last seen at
222 West Marble Street.

He has a white face
and a white tail.
His name is Spinner.

If you find him, please call
the Viras at 555-7123.
We will pay you a reward!

◆ **Circle the right answer.**

1. What kind of writing is this?

   a birthday card   a sign   a newspaper

2. What is the sign for?

   to find a lost dog   to sell a dog   to give a dog a home

3. What does **reward** mean?

   a paper saying you are bad   something given for doing a good deed

4. What kind of dog is lost?

Betty Bunny

It was early morning. Betty Bunny awoke to a noise. Something was in her kitchen! She was frightened.

Could it be mice? Crash! Bang! Clang! Then she heard a creak on the stair. Slowly her door opened.

It was the baby bunnies! They had cooked her breakfast!

◆ **Circle the right answer.**

1. What does **frightened** mean?

   afraid   happy   sleepy

2. When did this story happen?

   early morning   at lunchtime   late at night

3. Where was Betty when she heard a noise?

4. What did Betty think was making the noise?

Evan and Ken

Evan and Ken wanted to play store.
But they did not have any play money.

Evan said, "We can make our own money!"
He got paper and markers. He got out
scissors and old magazines too.

Evan and Ken cut out some dollars.
They pasted funny magazine pictures
where the face goes. They had so
much fun, they forgot to play store.

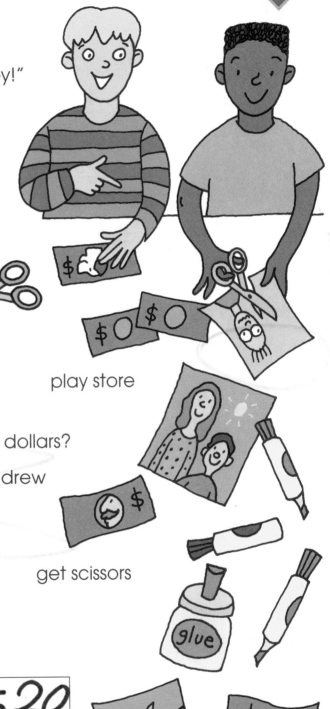

◆ **Circle the right answer.**

1. What did Evan and Ken want to do?

   read magazines   color pictures   play store

2. What did they use for the faces on their dollars?

   magazine pictures   pictures they drew

3. What did Evan and Ken forget to do?

   play store   make play money   get scissors

◆ **Draw your own play money.**

Drawing Conclusions

I'm Mad!

Dear Jonathan,

I'm mad at you. Who says girls cannot play soccer? I can play soccer better than any boy! You know it. I defeat you every time.

The Soccer Club should not be just for boys. A club like that is not nice and not fair. I bet it was Steven's idea. I thought we were friends.

Not your best friend,
Lizzie

◆ **Circle the right answer.**

1. Who made Lizzie mad?

   (Jonathan)   Steven   her mother

2. What did Lizzie think was not fair?

   The club was Steven's idea.   The club was for boys only.

3. What does **defeat** mean?

   help   work with   beat

◆ **Pretend you are Jonathan. Write a note back to Lizzie.**

Dear Lizzie,

I'm sorry I hurt your feelings. Would you like to be the first girl in our club?

Your friend,
Jonathan

Cindy!!!!

Native Americans

Native Americans means first Americans. American Indians are Native Americans. They were the first to live in this country.

Many Native Americans were hunters. They hunted deer or buffalo. Others were farmers. They grew corn, tomatoes or potatoes.

Nobody knows when the first Native Americans came to this country. But Native Americans have lived here for thousands of years.

◆ Draw a line to the end of each sentence.

1. **Native Americans** means   Native Americans came to this country.

2. Nobody knows when the first   were hunters.

3. Many Native Americans   first Americans.

◆ Circle the right answer.

4. What did some Native Americans hunt?

5. What did some Native Americans grow?

Cooking

Kids can cook wonderful foods! Some kids cook French toast for breakfast. Some kids cook flour tortillas for dinner. Lots of kids can cook soup for lunch.

How do kids learn to cook? They learn from their parents. They read about cooking in books. But kids should not learn to cook alone.

All good cooks are careful. Kid cooks should not cook without a grown-up to help. They know cooking is not playing.

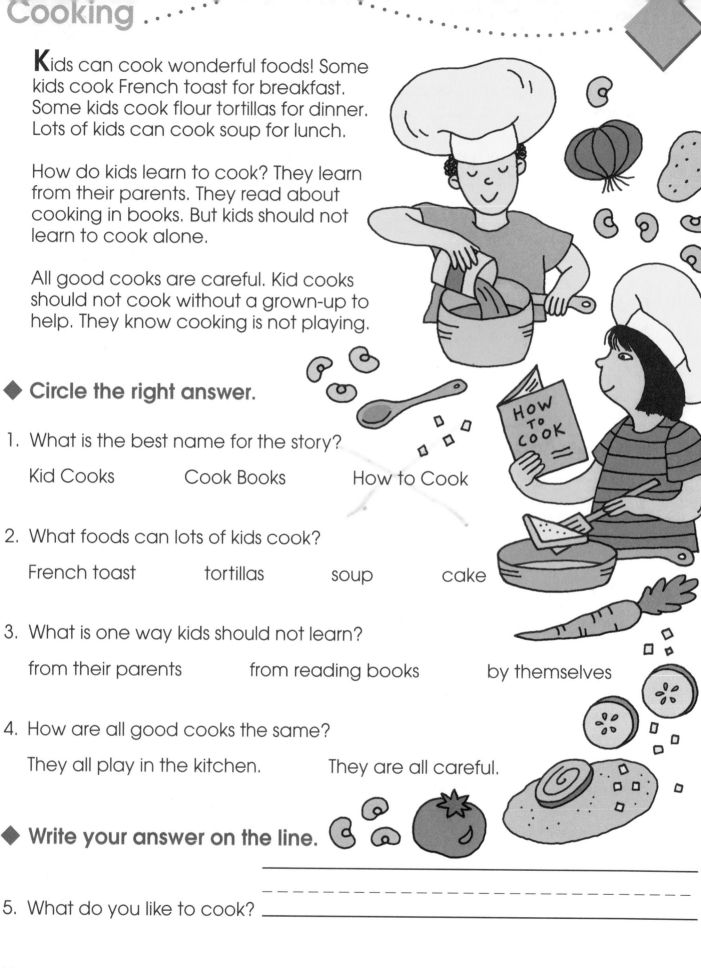

◆ **Circle the right answer.**

1. What is the best name for the story?

   Kid Cooks   Cook Books   How to Cook

2. What foods can lots of kids cook?

   French toast   tortillas   soup   cake

3. What is one way kids should not learn?

   from their parents   from reading books   by themselves

4. How are all good cooks the same?

   They all play in the kitchen.   They are all careful.

◆ **Write your answer on the line.**

5. What do you like to cook? _____

_____

Making Inferences

Pink Day!

When Kim went outside, the world had changed. Everything was pink! The sky was pink. The houses were pink. Even the grass was pink!

Kim did not like what she saw. Pink children were playing on pink sidewalks. Pink cars were driving on pink streets.

Then Kim remembered. She had on her PINK sunglasses. She took them off, and the world was back to normal.

◆ **Circle the right answer.**

1. What is the best name for the story?

   Pink Shoes   Kim Sees Pink   Kim Goes Walking

2. What was the problem?

   Everything was pink.   Kim went outside.

   Children were on sidewalks.   Cars were on streets.

3. What did Kim do to make the world look okay?

   She went back outside.   She took off her sunglasses.

4. What does **normal** mean?

   the way things usually are   a strange and new way

Jumping Chant

Flowers in the garden.
Flowers by the walk.
Flowers in the forest.
I wish they could talk.

Flowers dancing in the wind
and sprouting up in May.
If I met a flower friend,
what would I have to say?

◆ **Circle the right answer.**

1. What kind of writing is this?

   a letter   a story   a poem

2. What do flowers do in the wind?

   grow   dance   talk

3. What does **sprouting up** mean?

   getting planted   starting to grow

◆ **Draw a line to the word that rhymes.**

4. walk   shower

5. May   talk

6. flower   say

7. wish   fish

For Sale!

BUY MY BIKE!

Buy my spectacular bike!
It's a red and blue racer.
It has 10 speeds.

The bike is only 1 year old. It has
new tires and a new chain.

I will sell my bike for $50.
I need the money to go to camp.
Call Thomas at 555-9876.

◆ Circle the right answer.

1. Is this a sign to sell a bike?   **yes**   no

2. Does the bike belong to Thomas?   **yes**   no

3. Does Thomas want you to go to camp?   **yes**   no

4. Does the bike have new tires?   **yes**   no

5. Is the bike 10 years old?   **yes**   no

6. Does the bike cost $50?   **yes**   no

7. Does **spectacular** mean **really old and ugly**?   yes   **no**

The Brick House

The wolf was gone. The three pigs were safe together. They wanted to live in the brick house, but the house was too small.

They would add on to the house. Each pig would make a new bedroom. No pig would be lazy this time. All of the pigs would use bricks, not hay or straw. They would be ready if a wolf came again.

◆ **Circle the right answer.**

1. What is the best name for the story?

   A House for Three Pigs   Meet the Wolf!   We Can Be Lazy!

2. What was wrong with the brick house?

   It was too big.   It was too small.   It was too lazy.

3. What would the pigs do to fix it?

   make bedrooms   make bricks   be lazy

4. What does **lazy** mean?

   not willing to work   too silly to play   working too hard

5. Why would the pigs use bricks again?

   in case a wolf came again   in case they felt lazy later

314   Recalling Ideas/Sequencing

Scary Sink

Julie ran into the yard. "Mom, come quick!" she said. "There is a snake under the sink!"

Mom dropped the hose. She rushed in. There WAS a snake under the sink! She pushed it with a broom.

Alex ran in. "That's my toy snake," he laughed. Mom and Julie laughed too.

◆ **Circle the right answer.**

1. What scared Julie?

2. Where did Julie find the snake?

   in the yard   under the sink   under her bed

3. What did Mom use to get the snake?

4. Why did Alex laugh?

   Mom was trying to help.   The snake was just a toy.

Free Ticket!

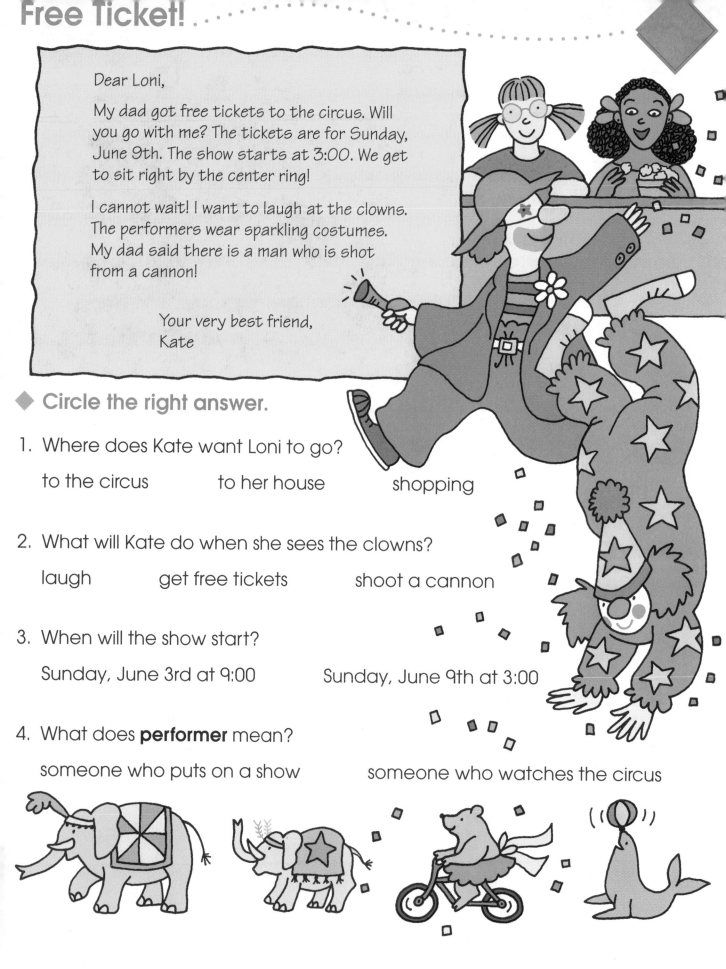

Dear Loni,

My dad got free tickets to the circus. Will you go with me? The tickets are for Sunday, June 9th. The show starts at 3:00. We get to sit right by the center ring!

I cannot wait! I want to laugh at the clowns. The performers wear sparkling costumes. My dad said there is a man who is shot from a cannon!

Your very best friend,
Kate

◆ **Circle the right answer.**

1. Where does Kate want Loni to go?

   to the circus   to her house   shopping

2. What will Kate do when she sees the clowns?

   laugh   get free tickets   shoot a cannon

3. When will the show start?

   Sunday, June 3rd at 9:00   Sunday, June 9th at 3:00

4. What does **performer** mean?

   someone who puts on a show   someone who watches the circus

In an Emergency

If you have an emergency, ask a grown-up to help. If you cannot find a grown-up, call **911**. People at **911** will help you be safe. They will help you fix what is wrong. Just push **911** on a telephone.

When **911** answers, tell that person your name. Tell where you live and what is wrong. Then listen carefully. The **911** person will tell you what to do next.

Never call **911** if nothing is wrong. People at **911** are busy helping people who need help right away.

◆ **Circle the right answer.**

1. What is the best name for the story?

   Calling Mom   Call 911   Telephone Games

2. What should you **NEVER** do?

   call 911 when nothing is wrong   look for a grown-up

3. What does **emergency** mean?

   a happy time at your home   a problem that needs help quickly

◆ **Write 1, 2, 3 and 4 to show the right order.**

4. _____ Listen carefully for what you should do next.

5. _____ Call 911.

6. _____ Try to find a grown-up.

7. _____ Tell your name, where you live and what is wrong.

In the Sky!

Sky Boy could fly. He lived in the sky. He used clouds for his bed and played tag with the birds. He played sky games all day long.

Sky Boy could slide down rays of the sun. He could ride on the wind like a kite. He took showers in the rain and rode around on tornadoes.

Sky Boy had one job that he loved. He painted the rainbows after it rained. That was more fun than all of his games.

◆ **Circle the right answer.**

1. What is the best name for the story?

   Rainbows   Sky Boy   Playing in the Rain

2. Can Sky Boy fly?   yes   no

3. Can Sky Boy paint?   yes   no

4. Can Sky Boy make it rain?   yes   no

5. Does Sky Boy play with birds?   yes   no

6. Does Sky Boy play slide in the rain?   yes   no

◆ **Unscramble the words to answer the question.**

7. What was Sky Boy's favorite thing to do?   tnpai a rbaoinw

   _____

   _

   _____

Answer Key

Page 289
1. I'm the Best Me!
2. wiggle
3. really great
4. buzz

Page 290
1. My Bones Are Missing!
2. write letters
3. Dog used them.
4. not think about what you do
5. letter picture, bone picture

Page 291
1. a cat who writes and draws
2. yes
3. no
4. yes
5. cat at computer

Page 292
1. Henry's Dream
2. a lion chasing him
3. in the jungle
4. a bad dream
5. was red.
6. were always white.
7. changed color too.

Page 293
1. a note
2. Kris
3. Jackie's friend
4. shoot
5. Tuesdays
6. very good

Page 294
1. from their bones
2. what size they were
3. their color
4. all over the world
5. middle dinosaur

Page 295
1. Make a Telephone
2. a telephone
3. in the bottom of both cups
4. in both ends of the string

Answers will vary.

Page 296
1. every day
2. cookies
3. very big
4. door
5. please

Page 297
1. Bad Robot!
2. forget
3. what Ben tells him
4. to say you did something wrong
5. by doing what Ben said not to do
6. scold
7. forgot
8. to

Page 298
1. in a newspaper
2. Lincoln School Wins!
3. read books
4. a prize

Answers will vary.

Page 299
1. an ad
2. at a pet store
3. dog shampoo
4. very quickly
5. dog baths

Page 300
1. Snake Soup
2. noodle soup
3. a little
4. snakes
5. Grandma
6. ladle picture on right

Page 301
1. a note
2. next week
3. maple, oak, elm
4. keep it green
5. picture of people planting trees

Page 302
1. shoe
2. chose the one you wanted
3. baseball

Answers will vary.

Page 303
1. yes
2. no
3. no
4. you find out if you can join
5. Giraffe's Idea
6. draw dancers

Page 304
1. Goodnight Sky
2. the sun
3. bright
4. the moon
5. Creeps
6. Flies

Answer Key

Answer Key

Page 305
1. a sign
2. to find a lost dog
3. something given for doing a good deed
4. black dog with a white face and tail

Page 306
1. afraid
2. early morning
3. bed
4. mice

Page 307
1. play store
2. magazine pictures
3. play store

Answers will vary.

Page 308
1. Jonathan
2. The club was for boys only.
3. beat

Answers will vary.

Page 309
1. first Americans.
2. Native Americans came to this country.
3. were hunters.
4. buffalo
5. corn

Page 310
1. Kid Cooks
2. soup
3. by themselves
4. They are all careful.
5. Answers will vary.

Page 311
1. Kim Sees Pink
2. Everything was pink.
3. She took off her sunglasses.
4. the way things usually are

Page 312
1. a poem
2. dance
3. starting to grow
4. talk
5. say
6. shower
7. fish

Page 313
1. yes
2. yes
3. no
4. yes
5. no
6. yes
7. no

Page 314
1. A House for Three Pigs
2. It was too small.
3. make bedrooms
4. not willing to work
5. in case a wolf came again

Page 315
1. snake
2. under the sink
3. broom
4. The snake was just a toy.

Page 316
1. to the circus
2. laugh
3. Sunday, June 9th at 3:00
4. someone who puts on a show

Page 317
1. Call 911
2. call 911 when nothing is wrong
3. a problem that needs help quickly
4. 4
5. 2
6. 1
7. 3

Page 318
1. Sky Boy
2. yes
3. yes
4. no
5. yes
6. no
7. paint a rainbow

Big Phonics Pencil Pal 08254